THE TWO LAWYERS:

A STORY FOR THE TIMES

BY

HENRY CLAY MORRISON

First Fruits Press
Wilmore, Kentucky
c2014

The Two Lawyers: A Story for the Times by Henry Clay Morrison

Published by First Fruits Press, © 2014
Previously Published by the Pentecostal Publishing Company, 1898

Digital version at http://place.asburyseminary.edu/firstfruitsheritagematerial/78/

ISBN: 9781621711537 (print), 9781621711544 (digital)

Morrison, H. C. (Henry Clay), 1857-1942.
The two lawyers : a story for the times / by H.C. Morrison.
240 p. : 21 cm
Wilmore, Ky. : First Fruits Press, c2014.
Reprint. Previously published: Louisville, Ky. : Pentecostal Pub. Co., c1898.
ISBN: 9781621711537 (pbk.)
1. Methodism -- Fiction. 2. Legal stories. 3. Attorneys -- Fiction. I. Title.
PZ1 .M67 2014   244

Cover design by Haley Hill

First Fruits Press
The Academic Open Press of Asbury Theological Seminary
204 N. Lexington Ave., Wilmore, KY 40390
859-858-2236
first.fruits@asburyseminary.edu
asbury.to/firstfruits

THE TWO LAWYERS:

A STORY FOR THE TIMES.

BY

REV. H. C. MORRISON,

EDITOR AND EVANGELIST.

Ninth Thousand.

———————

1898:
THE PENTECOSTAL PUB. CO. (INC.)
LOUISVILLE, KY.

PREFACE.

Unexpectedly to me, "The Two Lawyers" has materialized into a book. It was furthest from my thoughts that this would be the case when I commenced to write the chapters for the *Pentecostal Herald*.

The reader will readily see that there are some fillings of fiction woven into the warp of facts. We can safely say, however, that the facts contained in this book are stranger than the fiction in it.

H. C. MORRISON,
Evangelist and Editor

THE TWO LAWYERS.

A STORY OF THE TIMES.

CHAPTER I.

THE WATERS TROUBLED.

The city of Newton was a place of about twenty-five thousand population. It was situated in a fine region of country in one of the border states.

Its people, in their politics, education, manners and sentiments, were Southern. Newton, for a place of its size, was well abreast of the times. It enjoyed the advantages of the modern conveniences, such as electric lights, water-works, electric cars, brick-paved streets, excellent schools, and beautiful church buildings.

Most all of the evangelical denominations were represented in Newton, but the Southern Methodist Church predominated there.

The Southern Methodists had four congregations in Newton, one of them was merely a mission, two were very good second-class appointments, but Central Church had the largest edifice and the largest membership of any church in the city.

The register of this church contained some seven

hundred names. Some of the people, however, whose names were on the register were dead, some had moved away, a few had joined other denominations, and not a few had been lost sight of.

There were living in Newton, and in the country immediately around the city, at the time of which I write, not less than five hundred and seventy-five persons who recognized themselves as members of Central Church. This church had for many years enjoyed the distinction of having for its pastor a transfer. There were quite a number of preachers in the conference of which this charge was the first appointment, so far as number of members and the amount of money paid the preacher is concerned, who were quite competent to have filled its pulpit, but, unwisely, we think, the bishops had for some years humored this people by supplying them with a transfer.

To tell the simple truth there were two qualifications absolutely necessary for any man who might hope for a cordial reception as pastor of this congregation. He must be a *transfer*, and he must be a *doctor* of *divinity*.

At the time of which I speak, Newton had not enjoyed a genuine spiritual awakening for many years. There were middle-aged people in the church who had never heard any one shout because of spiritual ecstasy, and the young people of the congregation knew almost absolutely nothing of real Methodism. The fact is, the membership of this church was for the most part a very worldly people.

Quite a number of the official members attended the races, seemingly without any sort of compunc_ tions of conscience. To deal in futures was looked upon by not a few of them as legitimate business, and, I am sorry to say, several official members owned race horses, while two of them, who were the largest grocers in Newton, kept in their stores, and boldly displayed in their windows, all kinds of fine wines.

Dancing, card-playing, and theater-going were so common among the young people of the congregation that anyone who would have dared to have questioned the propriety of such behavior would have at once been put down as a religious fanatic.

Notwithstanding all this there were in Central Church some excellent people, of solid sense, and sterling character, some of whom had been soundly converted in the years gone by, and were grieved in their hearts over the spiritual apathy that possessed Newton. Among the humbler people there were those who were hungering and thirsting after righteousness, and as the years went by a few faithful women called earnestly upon God to send to the church and city a revival of "the old-time religion."

There were in the official board of Central

Church two men with whom this story has especially
to do. They were law-partners, and stood at the
head of their profession in the city of Newton.

One of them, William Hicks, was a man about
fifty-seven years of age, of medium-size, with
intelligent face and good natural ability, which
had been developed by some thirty-five years
practice of law. Hicks was a conscientious, pains-
taking, hardworking lawyer, and while he was
a modest man, making no pretentions, he was
recognized as one of the very safest men in
the State with whom to intrust an important
case.

Some people have an idea that a man can not
be a lawyer and a Christian; this is evidently a mistake. No doubt the life of a lawyer is one beset
with many and peculiar temptations, and yet a man
can be a lawyer and at the same time be a Christian,
and in a true and noble sense serve his generation
and follow Christ.

William Hicks' life was a practical demonstration
of the truth of the above statement.

Mr. George Mason Huton, Mr. Hicks' law partner, was a man forty-five years of age. He was
a man of intelligence and culture, possessed of
high moral convictions and noble impulses. He
had grown up in a quiet country home, the child of
pious parents. His mother came of old Methodist

stock, and for many years enjoyed and testified to the experience of perfect love.

Huton left home when quite young to attend college. On quitting college, he entered Mr. Hicks' law office. where he read law, and after being admitted to the bar had become a partner of Mr. Hicks. The men had from the first been most intimate and genuine friends. Their integrity and talents had, with earnest application, won financial success, and a good name among their fellowmen. When Huton's mother died he was deeply moved, and went so far as to unite himself with the Methodist Church, although he was not converted, which fact he knew full well, and often deeply deplored.

Hicks and Huton were anxious for the welfare of the church, and liberal with their money.

At the time when our story begins Rev. Josiah Poolkins, D. D., was pastor of Central Church. It was in the late spring of the second year of his pastorate. He was what is known in Methodism as "a two year man."

The only thing remarkable about Dr. Poolkins was the fact that somehow with but small ability as pastor or preacher, and with no reputation for zeal or piety, he had ingratiated himself with the appointing power, and notwithstanding the churches which he served were never built up under his ministry, somehow he managed to get himself trans-

ferred about from conference to conference, **and**
stationed in the best appointments. If Dr. Poolkins
excelled his brethren in anything, it was perhaps his
hatred of the old Methodist doctrine of entire
sanctification.

He seemed to believe the holiness movement was
the special calamity of the times. and while he put
forth no special effort against the whiskey traffic,
or other great vices of the times, and seemed to be
almost entirely indifferent to the worldliness which.
like a flood, had swept in upon the church, he embraced every possible opportunity to strike a vicious
blow at the holiness people, whom he took special
pleasure in calling, "second blessingists." When
the conversation which is recorded below took place,
Dr. Poolkins was delivering a series of sermons on
what he called, "The Holiness Craze." The Doctor
rarely preached without making some sort of a cut
at the holiness people, but just at this time he was
devoting special attention to the subject. It was
after the first one of these sermons, when our two
lawyers met in their law office one Monday morning,
that Hicks said to Huton:

HICKS: "How did you like the sermon yesterday
morning?"

HUTON: "I did not like it at all. I do not see
why our pastor should be all the time fighting holiness, or the 'second blessing,' as he calls it. He has

been pecking away on the holiness people almost constantly. If there is anybody in our church who professes sanctification, I do not know who it is, and there is nothing visible now that would indicate the near outbreak of religious fanaticism among us."

HICKS: "Who has been converted in our church since the present incumbent took charge of the pulpit about two years ago?"

HUTON: "Nobody, that I know of. You ought to be posted on such matters; you keep the church register."

HICKS: "Well, sir, we have not had a conversion since he came to us. I am the treasurer of the church, and keep an eye on the register, and know who's who, and there has been nobody converted in our church for over two years. During that time we have spent in church repairs, pastor's salary, and conference collections more than twelve thousand dollars, and not a soul saved."

HUTON: "Well, I think if the parson would smoke fewer cigars, tell fewer anecdotes, and fight sin instead of holiness, it would be better for us all. I am nothing to brag on myself, but I believe the Bible, and I believe there is going to be a Judgment day, and I can't see how the parson is going to face it with his head up."

HICKS: "The worst feature of it all is, his statements are not correct. You see, my wife's father was a Methodist preacher, and his old books are in my house, and I have been reading them of late, and all of our pastor's talk about the doctrine of the second blessing being a new heresy in the Church is nonsense. The Wesleys taught the doctrine, and their followers professed the experience long before the Methodist Church had an existence as a separate organization."

HUTON: "Say, did you notice yesterday that in the first part of his sermon he said it was a 'modern heresy,' but before he got through, he said John Wesley did teach it in early life, but in his riper years he changed his mind, and gave it up? That was an admission in itself that it is no new thing. If John Wesley taught it in early life, how can it be a new heresy?"

HICKS: "Oh, well, all his talk about John Wesley changing his mind on the subject has no foundation in fact. John Wesley urged his preachers to preach this doctrine to the close of his life. Then, look at the Bishop's address at the General Conference of 1894. It shows very plainly that we do not teach that men are sanctified when they are converted."

HUTON: "Why don't you tell him that he does not know what he is talking about?"

HICKS: "I hate to do that; wife has been wanting me to call him down, but I shall let the fellow alone."

HUTON: "Well, if you will let me have the books, so that I can post myself, I will let him have it straight. I am tired of this everlasting fight he is making on the holiness people."

HICKS: "I will bring the books down to the office to-morrow."

HUTON: "All right. I will post myself, and surprise him some day when he is lounging about our office."

CHAPTER II.

AT CLOSE QUARTERS.

Two weeks later, when the law-partners met in their office on Monday, the following conversation took place:

HUTON: "Well, I have been reading up on those books you let me have week before last, and must confess I am surprised at their contents. I had no idea the doctrine of entire sanctification as a work of grace subsequent to regeneration, was so clearly taught in our history and standards. I can not understand how our pastor can make the statements he has, and does, with these facts before him."

HICKS: "Possibly he never read them."

HUTON: "I hardly see how that could be; he has evidently read the course of study, and he has two capital D's attached to his name. I can hardly excuse him on the ground of ignorance, but I would hate to believe that he would wilfully misrepresent plain facts."

HICKS: "Why don't you sound him, and find out whether it is *ignorance* or *dishonesty?*"

HUTON: "That is just what I intend to do. I have been waiting for him to get through with the matter. You see, he was still hammering away on it in yesterday's sermon. Did you notice in yesterday's sermon there was a hint of approval of Samuel P.

Wright's views? He said the time was coming when patience would cease to be a virtue, and the Church must be purged of those elements that disturbed its peace. I told him I wanted him to drop into the office some time this week, that I wanted to talk with him about some points of doctrine and else."

HICKS: "Well sir, yonder he comes — now keep cool, and do thorough work if you raise the question at all."

Enter Pastor. — "Good-morning, brethren, how are you this morning? Well, Brother Huton, you said you wanted to have a talk with me on doctrine when I had leisure. Monday is sort of an off day, and I thought I would drop in and see what I can do for you."

HUTON: "Yes; I am glad you came in. I have been much interested in your recent sermons on the 'modern holiness craze,' and I wanted to ask you with regard to a few points."

POOLKINS: "I have been thoroughly posting myself on the subject, and hope I may be able to answer your questions."

HUTON: "By the way, I noticed in your sermon yesterday that you heartily endorse certain parties in Texas, in their suggestion as to the best method of getting rid of the so-called holiness movement in our church. That is, expel from the min-

istry and membership all of our pastors who hold to
the Wesleyan view."

POOLKINS: "I do most heartily approve of the
Texas suggestion. I do not like your way of putting it, however. I would say, 'all second blessingists,' and not 'all who hold to the Wesleyan view
You know, in these matters, we must be a little
careful how we frame our sentences, and be guarded
in our use of terms."

HUTON: "Well, in order to get rid of them, we
would have to put out the local preachers also: many
of them you know profess this blessing."

POOLKINS: "Oh, well, when we got rid of all the
cranky itinerants, most of the local preachers mixed
up in the craze would go out with them."

HUTON: "I suppose that would be true of the
weaker element, but there are some of them that
you would have to try and expel."

POOLKINS: "That is true, no doubt, but when
Bishop, Presiding Elder and Pastor are all one
against him, we can make short work of a cranky
local preacher. Oh, you need have no fears, those
things have all been thought over, and can be managed easily."

HUTON: "What about the laymen? Scores of them
are infected with these doctrines. They will rent
halls, fit up empty stores, and fill the woods with holi-
nesss camp-meetings; what will you do with them?"

POOLKINS: "Well, they ought to be made to walk the plank with their gang. I do not know just how the brethren propose to manage all these details. I suppose the brethren of Texas have thought out some plan. They would hardly have proposed the thing without thinking over the feasibility of it."

HUTON: "I see, but had you thought that you will have to change the course of study for young preachers, or the Annual Conference will be one constant series of trial for heresy?"

POOLKINS: "That will be easy to do."

HUTON: "True enough, but there would yet remain an embarrassing feature in this purging process."

After a long pause, in which the pastor showed much nervousness, he looked over at Huton and said thoughtfully, "To what do you refer?"

HUTON: "The book burning."

POOLKINS: "What book burning do you refer to?"

HUTON: "Oh, the old Methodist books: Standards, histories, biographies, disciplines, hymn books, old magazines, and newspapers. You see if the anti-Wesleyan element in our church should undertake such a course of persecution as you and some of your brethren advocate, it would arouse tremendous interest, and thousands of people, who have thought but little on the subject, would go to reading the old Methodist books. And if they did, you brethren would be in a bad box on your heresy dodge. There is one feature that I doubt if you had thought of. All these hundreds and thousands of pastors, local preachers, and laymen that you propose to turn out of the church are well supplied with the old Methodist books, and they will be constantly proving to the world from the plainest statements, in which these books abound, that you men are the heretics, and that they are the true church. It is more than likely that they will take the matter into the courts, and if they should, these old books would ruin you there. My counsel to you, as a lawyer, would be, before you undertake to put anybody out of the church on your wild Texas plan, get all of the old Methodist books in your hands, and burn the whole business. It would be a sight to behold. You orthodox, truly loyal savers of church and country, burning "Wesley's Sermons," "Watson's Institutes," "Clarke's Commentaries," and all the rest, old disciplines, and standard hymn books."

POOLKINS: "I deny that the old Methodist books teach second blessingism. I challenge any man to find it in them."

HUTON: "Now, Dr. Poolkins, I advise you to move carefully. I hardly know how I got into the church. I know I never was converted, never have claimed to be, but I love the Methodist Church. My mother, a plain country woman, lived and died in it. She was what you call a second blessingist, and if ever a saint lived on earth she was one. For that reason, when you commenced your war on the second blessing people, I was especially interested. My law partner here, Brother Hicks, has a large collection of the old Methodist books, and I have borrowed and read them much of late, and I take issue with you as to the teachings contained in them. Yesterday, you remember, you threw your glove in the arena. That is the reason I asked you around here this morning. I want to tell you that I take it up and will be glad to debate the subject with you."

POOLKINS: "Well, brother, you of course understand that I made that challenge for some of the second blessing leaders. I would not think of debating with you on the subject."

HUTON: "Yes you will, Dr. Poolkins. You have stood in the pulpit of our church Sabbath after Sabbath, misrepresenting facts, berating the holiness people, and challenging any man, all comers, to answer you, and now I propose to do it, and you can not afford to back down."

POOLKINS: "I did not come here to be insulted, and tell you once for all, that I will not debate with you."

HUTON: "I do not propose to insult you, but you

Sabbath, and now you must meet me in debate on the subject. If you will not, I will write up the whole matter for the press, and not only that, Doctor, but you know the District Conference elected me to our next Annual Conference, and I will object to the passing of your character.'

POOLKINS: "On what grounds will you object to the passing of my character, sir?"

HUTON: "I will have you arrested for the misrepresentation of facts. I will prove that your statements on the subject that you have been discussing have been wilfully false, then you can take the consequences, or save yourself by establishing your *ignorance.* I will have the *books* present, and we will have the facts all brought out in a clear, strong light Now, you can meet me in open debate, publicly confess that your statements are not correct, and take your *gloves* out of the arena, or have your character arrested this fall at the Annual Conference. I will give you any reasonable length of time to make up your mind with regard to the course you wish to pursue."

CHAPTER III.
DETERMINED TO PRESS THE BATTLE.

Dr. Poolkins left the office of lawyers Huton and Hicks a crestfallen man. He knew that Huton was a bright, genial man, a good lawyer, a splendid speaker, prosperous in his business, and liberal with his money, always ready to give for the enterprises of the church; but he knew that Huton did not have family prayer, and that when he took charge of the church, Huton laughingly said to him: "Doctor, you may count on me to pay, but you must not call on me to pray," to which he had very readily agreed, saying: "Well, my brother, it takes money to make things go." Huton was the last man on earth Dr. Poolkins would have expected to stand up in defense of the holiness people; knowing that Huton's piety, if he was really a Christian at all, was at a very low ebb, he naturally supposed that Huton would heartily endorse all he had said, or would say against the holiness people. Huton had paid one hundred dollars a year on his salary, and he had enjoyed dropping into his office to chat, read the papers, and have a pleasant hour; and now that Huton had challenged him to debate, and threatened to arrest his character, he hardly knew what to do.

The Doctor had been having fair sailing. Many people in his church belonged to the first social and dancing parties were of weekly occurrence among the young people of his church, and the doctor had thought that if there was a place on earth where a man could, unhindered, vent his spleen against the old Wesleyan doctrine of entire sanctification, with the hearty approval of all his congregation, he was occupying that place. The experience of the morning had been as unexpected and startling as a clap of thunder out of a clear sky. The doctor's only hope was that Huton did not really mean what he said.

"Surely he will not press this matter to an issue: he seemed good natured, in fact was laughing all the time he was talking to me; I do wonder if he was playing a practical joke on me. But, what if he should be in earnest? My only hope would be to transfer. How could I fix that up, with my wife in good health? My throat was sore once at a very opportune time, but my voice is as clear as a bell now." Thus the doctor went musing on his way. There was silence in the office of the two lawyers for some time after the preacher left. Hicks spoke first -"Huton, you really did not mean what you said this morning, did you?"

HUTON: "I did most assuredly mean every word of it. That man must stand up in the pulpit and correct his statements, or meet me in public debate and substantiate what he has said, or have his char

acter arrested at the next Annual Conference. I
have thought it all over carefully. I have had all
three of his sermons on the ' Modern Holiness Craze,'
taken down verbatim by my stenographer, and I am
amazed at the man. He has presumed on the great
want of spiritual life, the general ignorance of
Methodist history and doctrine among our people,
and has talked in a most reckless manner. Why,
Hicks, there would be just as much truth and sense
in you getting up at a Fourth of July celebration and
saying that George Washington, in his old age,
repudiated American independence, as there is in
Dr. Poolkins saying that John Wesley repudiated
the doctrine of entire sanctification. You had just
as well call Mark Twain the *father* of his country as
to call any modern evangelist or pastor the father
of the 'new heresy of second blessingism.' Hicks,
you heard me tell our pastor this morning that I
have never been converted; well, it is a sad fact, but
do you know I have prayed more in the last three
weeks, since I have been reading those old Methodist books, than I have before in the past ten years.
I tell you a man can not read our standards of doctrine with peace if sin is in his life. I have had half
a mind to rent a hall and send off and get some holiness evangelist to come here and hold a meeting,
and see if I can get converted. Then, there is my
wife, she is in no better condition than myself, and

our children, the three oldest are members of the church, but know nothing of a change of heart.

"We need some one to lead us to Christ; we do not understand these things, but, sir, if I should send and get an evangelist and rent a hall, and we should hold a meeting, and a hundred souls should be saved, it is quite probable the evangelist and myself would both be expelled from the church, and yet there has not been a conversion in our church for more than two years. It looks hard for a man to just sit still and go to perdition, and take his family with him."

HICKS: "Why don't you get down on your knees and ask Christ to save you, and then you could lead your family to Christ?"

HUTON: "It is easy to say that, my old friend, but it is quite another thing to do it. Why did not the Hebrews get together and go out of Egypt without Moses to lead them, and why did they not pass over Jordan without a Joshua to lead them? When a man is as far away from Christ as I am, and knows as little of Him as I do, he needs some fellow-being who knows Christ, and understands the way of approach to Him to lead him."

HICKS: "Well, Huton, I had no idea you were in such a state of mind. I know, and you know, my life has not been what it should have been, but such as my poor prayers are, you shall have the benefit of them."

HUTON: ''Oh, well, I had not thought of these things much until I commenced reading up on this holiness question, but Wesley's Sermons put me to thinking. I said to myself, if these things be true, who then can be saved?' and the trouble about it all is, they are *true*. I have not had a good night's sleep in a week, that is what I challenged that man to the debate for. I got up after midnight last night and prayed for two hours, and I promised God if he would forgive my sins I would defend His truth against misrepresentations.''

HICKS: ''That is not the way to get saved. You are trying to buy salvation, and pay for it in holding a debate with a holiness fighter. You will never make a landing in that way. Salvation, as I understand it, is 'giving and taking.' God gives, you take.''

HUTON: ''I wonder if there is a holiness meeting anywhere in this region of the country that a man could attend? Say, that woods of mine out there on the hill, just out of the city limits, would make a magnificent place for a camp-meeting.''

HICKS: ''It would be an ideal place; plenty of shade, and plenty of water. People could walk out from town, and two country roads cross right at the corner of the woods.''

HUTON: '' How much are you in for a holiness camp-meeting here next summer?''

HICKS: "I don't know, all that is necessary. Put me down $50 to begin with."

HUTON: "Good, that makes $100, as I will give $50, and I know a number of men in town and country who will contribute. There will be no trouble about raising the money. I will write at once to Evangelist Courage and see if he can come and hold the meetings for us."

HICKS: "By the way, have you seen the *Nashville Advocate* of February 24th? It contains a criticism on Rev. T. A. Kerley's book, 'Conference Rights,' from the editor."

HUTON: "No, I have not seen the paper, but I must have Kerley's book; it is — from what I hear of it — a book that our preachers and laymen should read. If a conference has rights it ought to know it. What does the editor of the *Advocate* say of the book?"

HICKS: "Well, what amused me is his reference to the Kelly - Hargrove case. Kerley treats this case in his book. The editor intimates that Kerley's treatment of the case is one-sided, and says, 'if we should conclude to make an explanation and defense, then we promise to make it so complete that no mere piecemeal censure will thereafter be in order.'"

HUTON: "Oh, that sounds exactly like him."

HICKS: "Yes, I said to my wife that he remin led me of a boastful boy. I have seen boys who w ould say, 'I could throw a big rock over the top of the church steeple, and jump over the river at one bound if I wanted to, but I don't want to.' The larger boys understand the situation and smile at each other; only the very small and very inexperienced little fellows really think they have found a hero, and they will soon get skeptical, if he does not perform some miracle of strength to show that he can make his boasts good."

HUTON: "I see. Yes, the doctor has intimated frequently that he has some sort of psychological shell convenient with which he can blow up the entire holiness movement, if he should really think it necessary. He made a mistake when he intimated that he could clear up the Kelly-Hargrove case so easily. These things were not done in a corner. If he has it in his power to put the matter in a clear, favorable light before the church, he ought by all means to do so. The truth is, Kerley's statements are correct, and the less said by the other side the better."

While this conversation was going forward in the office Dr. Poolkins was walking slowly and thoughtfully homeward. Just as he came to his yard-gate he met with Sister Dishrattler, one of the prominent women of the church, to whom he answered, when she inquired after the welfare of his family, "My wife is not looking very well, I really believe I ought to take her to some more congenial climate." Sister Dishrattler expressed great surprise, saying she had not noticed any indications of a decline in Mrs. Poolkins' health.

When the Doctor went into his house his wife said to him, "What did you mean by telling old Sister Dishrattler that I am in poor health? I never felt better in my life." "Yes, dear," said the doctor, "that is the way with you women; you will go as long as you can drag, and when it is too late you will admit that you are sick. I know you better than you know yourself, and I know you ought to have a change of climate."

"Well," said his wife, "I am sure I can't tell whatever put the notion into your head that I am sick, and need a change of climate."

"I do not say that you are sick, my dear," said the Doctor, "but your whole appearance indicates that you need a change, and I think one of my first duties is to save my wife's health at any sacrifice to myself. and I intend to write to Bishop Helper to-night and ask him if there is a *good* opening so that he could transfer us to some place in the South."

CHAPTER IV.

DR. POOLKINS LEAVES NEWTON.

Our last chapter closed with a conversation between Dr. Poolkins and his wife on the subject of the latter's health. That evening before retiring, Dr. Poolkins wrote the following letter:

"REV. BISHOP HELPER, D. D.

"*Dear Bishop:* It becomes my painful duty to write you with regard to my wife's poor health. Her condition is such that I can not afford to longer ignore her great need of a change of climate. I fear that to undertake to pass through the summer and winter with her in this region of many sudden and radical changes would be unwise. I believe that a few years in a warm climate would perhaps fully restore her health. I have no doubt you could readily secure some one to supply the pulpit which I now occupy until the meeting of the Annual Conference, which convenes only about four months from this date. Is there not an opening for me in some one of the Southern conferences? As I shall want to screen my wife as much as possible, I hope you can find me a church with a comfortable parsonage and a living salary. I could arrange to move on very short notice. I should be glad to get my wife away from this place just as soon as possible. If you have an opening now in mind, telegraph at once at my expense.

"Wishing you health and much happiness, and fruit in your great field of labor, I remain,

"Fraternally yours,

"JOSIAH POOLKINS."

The news was soon circulated about the town that Mrs. Poolkins was in very poor health, and that her husband would likely be compelled to transfer to some one of the Southern conferences, in order to get her into a mild climate before the rigors of winter came on. In the streets, at church, and at the parsonage, in fact everywhere Mrs. Poolkins went, persons were extending to her their sympathy because of her poor health, but trying to encourage her by telling her that she looked remarkably well. Our two lawyers could but exchange knowing glances at each other when they heard the matter of the transfer discussed.

Five days after Dr. Poolkins' letter was addressed to Bishop Helper, the following telegram was handed him:

"REV. JOSIAH POOLKINS:

"There is no place open. Will keep you in mind. My wife has written to your wife. I sympathize with you deeply.

"JOHN G. HELPER."

This was poor comfort for Dr. Poolkins, but he simply had to await developments.

On the Sabbath following Huton's acceptance of the challenge the Doctor seemed so subdued and meek in the pulpit that the marked change caused much comment. Sister Dishrattler hurried about the church as soon as the benediction was pronounced, to gossip with various groups of people about the poor pastor's distress with regard to his wife's health.

The truth was, that night after night, until toward midnight, for the past week, Poolkins had been poring over pages of Methodist history and standards of doctrine. He had read more really good literature in the past week than he had seen since he completed his Conference Course. He had become fully aware of the fact that he could not for a moment sustain the position he had assumed, and that almost all of the statements made in his three sermons on "The Modern Holiness Craze" were entirely out of harmony with the plain facts in the case.

The Doctor's only hope was a speedy transfer. He had preached most all of his star sermons any way, and it would soon be time for him to seek some other field for the display of his talents. So he determined to write to several other bishops for a transfer.

While Dr. Poolkins was out attending to some business Monday afternoon, and Sister Dishrattler was up at the parsonage trying to comfort Sister Poolkins over her poor health, and to find out any little thing about the preacher's family affairs that she did not already know, the letter came to Mrs. Poolkins from Mrs. Bishop Helper. It is unnecessary

to give address, dates, etc. The contents were as
follows:

"*My Dear Sister Poolkins:* You can not know how
grieved the Bishop and myself were to hear of your
poor health. The Bishop regretted very much that
there was no place just now in the South to which
he could transfer your husband, but thinks there
will be no trouble finding him a suitable appointment after the meeting of the fall conferences.
But we are not willing for your health to be sac-
rificed, and I hasten to write to you to come to me
at once. The Bishop leaves for an extended western
tour in a few days, and I will be here all alone,
except our two faithful servants. Our house is
large, and there is not a more healthful place in all
the Southland, and we will be only too glad to have
you. Besides, it will not cost you a cent, and the
Bishop is not willing for me to spend the fall and
winter alone. So I beg you, for my sake, as well as
your own, to come to me at once. It will not be
necessary to wait to answer this letter, or make
much preparation, but just come along, and take a
good rest. Dr. Poolkins can remain on his charge
until after his Conference, and then no doubt get a
transfer that will be suitable.

"With much love, I am devotedly yours,
                    "HANNAH M. HELPER."

Mrs. Poolkins opened the letter and read it aloud
to Sister Dishrattler, who was overjoyed that such
good news had come, and that she was the first to
hear it. She could hardly wait to hear the con-

clusion, so eager was she to spread the news over the town that their "dear pastor's sorrows were at an end, for Mrs. Bishop Helper had invited Sister Poolkins to spend the winter in her Southern home."

As the Doctor returned home he met Sister Dishrattler on the street, who, in the presence of two of his official board with whom he was talking over the sad necessity of his having to leave them, gave him the full contents of the letter which his wife had just received.

Dr. Poolkins was filled with indignation as he stood helpless while Sister Dishrattler poured out the news, and said that she would be up the next morning to help Sister Poolkins pack her trunks and make preparation for the journey.

Sister Dishrattler hurried on to spread the news. As the Doctor entered the house his wife met him with a radiant face, exclaiming, "Oh, Doctor, I have the most lovely letter from Mrs. Bishop Helper, asking me to spend some time with her."

POOLKINS: "Dear, why did you let Sister Dishrattler see that letter? half the people in town will know of it before dark."

MRS. POOLKINS: "Well, there does not seem to be any secret about it. I am eager to get away. I have been talked to so much about being sick that I am sure I will be sick if I do not leave this place. I have just had my trunk brought down, cleaned, and put in the hall. I expect to leave day after to-morrow. I would not be harassed about my health another week as I have been the last one for anything imaginable."

POOLKINS: "You would not go and leave me, would you, dear?"

MRS. POOLKINS: "I do not see why I should not go at once. You know I said from the first that my health was good, but you insisted to the contrary, and the whole town has joined with you, and it is a torture to remain here, so I will leave for the summerland day after to-morrow. You can come when it suits you. I have not had a nice trip in years, and I shall be off at once."

POOLKINS: "Well, wife, you know I will not permit you in your state of health to undertake such a journey by yourself."

MRS. POOLKINS: "I see no need whatever of your leaving your church; besides, Mrs. Helper did not ask us both to come. I do not know that it would be convenient for her to entertain both of us."

Poolkins said no more, but busied himself that evening packing his trunk, into which he put the manuscript of several of his most eloquent and learned sermons.

The poor man was sick at heart. He did not know what to do. He could but hope that his wife's poor health, and the general sympathy aroused for him on that account, would keep Huton from pressing the matter of the debate. In this the Doctor was badly mistaken. On the very morning of the day that Mrs. Bishop Helper's letter arrived, Lawyers Huton and Hicks had the following conversation:

HICKS: "Say, Huton, you will have to let that man off, now that his wife is sick, and my judgment is that you have silenced his battery against the holiness movement in these parts."

HUTON: "No; I will do nothing of the sort. I intend to teach him a lesson that will be a means of grace to himself and all of his kind. If Dr. Poolkins and those men in our church, who have departed from old Wesleyan Methodism, desire to assail those time-honored doctrines, let them do so; but they can not afford to follow their present methods. They must have the courage to make an open and bold attack, and not undertake to drive our real Methodist people out of the church with tne cry of 'heresy,' 'second blessingism,' 'disloyalty,' and the like. The whole thing is shamefully dishonest, and I can not see how a man can take the course which Poolkins has and retain self-respect. Here is a note I wrote him last night, which I wish to read you before sending it to him, and see what you think of it:

"'REV. JOSIAH POOLKINS, D. D.,

"'*Dear Sir and Brother:* You doubtless remember

the conversation we had in my office some days since, in which I accepted your challenge, so frequently made from our pulpit, to meet any man who would undertake to affirm that our church, in its history and standards of doctrine, teaches the second work of grace, or, as you prefer to call it, 'second blessingism.' I thought I made it clear to you that I cheerfully accept your challenge. Having heard nothing further from you, I drop you this note. Many persons who heard your sermons on the 'Modern Holiness Craze' are anxious that we have an open discussion on the subject. Please let me hear from you at once, that arrangements may be made for the debate to take place at the earliest date possible. Respectfully,

"'GEORGE HUTON.'"

The above note was sent to Dr. Poolkins, with directions to the boy to wait for an answer, with which he soon returned. It read as follows:

"HON. GEORGE HUTON,

"*Dear Sir and Brother:* Your note just received. My wife's health is such that she must at once leave for the South, and as I shall have to accompany her, and may be detained for some weeks looking after her comfort, it is impossible for me to go into arrangements for debate with you now on the subject mentioned in your note. I very much regret that it is out of my power at this time to discuss the subject before the public. Respectfully yours,

"JOSIAH POOLKINS."

On the evening of the same day that the above

notes were exchanged, the following notice appeared
in one of the evening papers:

"ATTENTION !

"On next Friday evening at the City Hall, in this
city, Hon. George Huton will address the people on
the subject of 'The Modern Holiness Craze.' Speaking will begin at 7:30 sharp. No admission fee.
Everybody is cordially invited.
                    "HON. WILLIAM HICKS,
                    "JUDGE JACOB HARDEE,
                    "EDITOR MALCOM SAUNDERS,
                        "Committee of Arrangements. ᾽

This notice created great interest in the city, and
intense excitement in Dr. Poolkins' church. It was
the theme of conversation in all circles of business
and society. Sister Dishrattler was in and out of
the parsonage, and up and down the streets, and
within a few hours after the notice had appeared in
the paper, had thoroughly posted herself with reference to all that had passed between Poolkins and
Huton, and had outstripped the newspapers in
spreading all of the details and particulars throughout the city. The newspapers took the matter up,
and it was discussed *pro* and *con.* Some said that
"Huton belonged to a clique who wished to drive
from the church one of the most learned and sweet-
spirited ministers the city had ever been blessed
with." Others contended that "laymen were as

much interested in the welfare of the church as
preachers were, and, as they had to pay, they had a
right to say, also." Many hundreds of people had
heard Dr. Poolkins' challenge, and while it never
occurred to them that anyone would accept it, they
could but feel that the Doctor ought to meet the
issue and defend the position he had taken.

At many a fireside it was whispered that Sister
Poolkins had found out that she was in need of a
change of climate at a very opportune time. So
strange, too, that just now, in the beautiful montns
of the early summer, they should be in such haste
to flee from the coming winter.

Poor Mrs. Poolkins, she could hardly hold up her
head. An awful suspicion knocked more than once
for admission at her heart's door, but her devotion
to, and confidence in her husband repelled it, tor
which let us feel thankful. for had she known the
whole truth she could but have loathed him.

On Thursday evening Dr. Poolkins and wife left
for the far South, but while they sat in the depot a
boy scattering dodgers handed them one announcing
Huton's speech to be delivered at the City Hall the
following evening.

Friday evening a great throng of people from
every part of the city might be seen wending their
way to the City Hall, which had been put in excei-
lent order by the committee of arrangements, who

were on hand with several ushers to seat the congregation.

When Huton entered he found every seat in the hall occupied, from pit to gallery, with many extra chairs which had been brought and placed in the aisles. The platform was occupied by the lawyers and city officials, and just in front of the speaker's stand were reporters of the two leading daily papers sharpening their pencils.

The audience did not see Huton until he ascended the platform and came forward to the speaker's desk, when a deathlike stillness fell over the vast assembly

CHAPTER V.

HUTON'S ADDRESS.

Huton stood in silence for a moment looking over the vast sea of upturned faces. He was a tall, broad-shouldered fellow, his chin and forehead showed great strength of character and intellect; his mouth indicated purpose, and his kindly eyes revealed at once the fact that his purpose was noble, unselfish, and pure.

The pause was broken with these words, "Let us pray." Every one who could do so went to their knees; those who could not kneel, bowed their heads in reverence. Lawyer Hicks led the prayer. It was the first time his voice had ever been heard in that city in prayer. His words were slow and full of emotion. He asked God that He would bless the meeting; that He would guide the speaker; that the old Methodist banner which had led the charge of the militant hosts in the rout of sin and Satan ten thousand times, might now be caught away from the hands of the enemies of Wesley and his co-adjutors, and borne back by hearts loyal and true to God and man to the head of the advancing column of the mighty holiness revival, in the hands of those who were willing to suffer reproach, if need be, for old doctrines that brought persecution and suffering in the days of Christ, Paul, and John Wesley.

At the close of the prayer there were a few verses of " Am I a Soldier of the Cross " sung by four young men on the platform, and then Huton came to the front of the platform and spoke as follows:

"*Ladies and Gentlemen, Brothers and Sisters:* It has been my duty and my privilege to speak on many occasions, and before many and varied audiences. I have represented you and your interests in various capacities, as mayor, councilman, and treasurer, and in the senate of our State; I have stood and plead in all of your courts, and before the Supreme Court of this great nation, but in all my past experience I have never realized so great a responsibility as that which rests upon me to-night. I most humbly ask for your sympathy, and your prayers.

" First of all, I will say that I am here to abuse no one: such is the least of my desire or intention. I am here to exercise the right which every American citizen enjoys, to speak out plainly in behalf, and in defense of what I believe to be the eternal and essential truths of the religion of Jesus Christ. The people of this audience are well acquainted with the circumstances which have led up to this meeting. As is well known, our pastor preached three sermons on what he was pleased to call the ' Modern Holiness Craze.' When the subject was first announced, I was deeply interested, and not only did I listen

closely to the series of sermons, but I had my
stenographer to take them down in shorthand and
reproduce them on the typewriter, and I have them
here on the desk before me, word for word, just as
they fell from Dr. Poolkins' lips. It is well known
that the Doctor gave his audience to understand
that his glove, and indeed, first and last, several
pairs of them, were in the arena, and he challenged
any and all men to produce a page, paragraph or
word of proof, from the Methodist doctrine or history, that could for a moment, even, be distorted into
a ' squint ' at the second blessing theory of sanctification. The Doctor's repeated challenges put me to
thinking, and firally to making a thorough investiga-
tion of facts as they really exist. I do not suppose I
used preachers' methods, but I went at it simply as a
lawyer, and hunted for evidence, just as I would in a
case coming before the courts. I found the evidence,
and shall produce some of it here — not all of it. for
that would detain you for many hours.

"I regret that Dr. Poolkins could not meet me
here and divide the time, but my remarks shall all
be taken down by a good stenographer, put in type,
and submitted to him for examination and answer at
any time he may desire.

"Before I proceed to discuss the subject, however,
I want to say in humility, and with deep gratitude,
that whatever unpleasant features there may be

connected with this agitation on the subject of sanctification, it has proved an inestimable blessing to
me. For many years I have been a member of the
church. I have been a firm believer in Methodist
doctrine and polity, and have always cheerfully contributed of my means to support its institutions;
but, with shame, I must confess that I had never been
converted.

"When I commenced reading our books of history and doctrine this fact which was constantly
kept before me, became so exceedingly painful that
I was forced frequently to lay down my books and
betake myself to my knees. With reading and
praying there was a deepening of conviction, until
it became so intense that I was unable longer to
endure the consciousness of guilt that was resting
upon me. Last Wednesday night, while at prayer-
meeting, I resolved not to sleep until my peace was
made with my Maker. So, leaving the church, I
went to my office where, on my knees, after midnight, in repentance, tears, and agony of soul, I was
made sweetly and clearly conscious of the fact that
all my sins were forgiven, that I was indeed a child
of God. I am now an humble seeker after the more
complete and perfect work, that I find taught in the
scriptures, in the standards of my church, and that I
know was found and enjoyed by my now sainted mother,
which Methodists call 'entire sanctification.'"

There was a murmur of applause and praise which swept over the audience, followed by a deathlike stillness as every one leaned forward eager to catch every word of the speaker.

"The question that I propose to ask and answer is this: Does the Methodist Church in her history, standards of doctrine, Discipline, and Hymn Book teach that there is a second work of grace, wrought of God in the believer's heart, subsequent to regeneration?

"It will be readily remembered by many persons in this audience, that Dr. Poolkins in the first of his three sermons on the 'Holiness Craze,' informed us that the 'second blessing doctrine' was a new heresy, which some fanatics are trying to foist upon our church; in his second sermon he contradicted these statements, however, by saying that John Wesley taught the second work of grace, but that he changed his views on the subject in his mature years. In his third sermon he accuses all who believe in the remains of sin in believers, and the necessity of the subsequent work of grace, of being heretics, and joins with Rev. Samuel P. Wright, of Texas, in suggesting their being deposed from the ministry.

"Now the plain, simple facts are that none of Dr. Poolkins' statements are correct.

"John Wesley did plainly teach that sin remains

in regenerated persons, and that it is removed in entire sanctification.

"He did not change his views on the subject. Hence the doctrine of the second work of grace, is not '*new*,' nor is it from a Methodist standpoint a *heresy*.

"I will quote a paragraph from one of Wesley's sermons preached in 1790, only ten months before his death:

"'Only let it be remembered that the heart, even of a believer, is not wholly purified when he is justified. Sin is overcome, but is not rooted out; it is conquered, but not destroyed. Experience shows him first, that the root of sin, self-will, pride and idolatry, remain still in his heart. But as long as he continues to watch and pray, none of them can prevail against him. Experience teaches him, secondly, that sin (generally pride or self-will) cleaves to his least actions. So that even with regard to these, he finds an absolute necessity for the blood of atonement.' Sermons, Vol. 2. Page 476.

"From this it is plain that John Wesley did not change his mind with reference to the remains of sin in the believer. Let it be borne in mind also, that the paragraph just read to you is selected from a standard of doctrine in our church. So it would seem that the theories of those men, who are opposing the holiness movement are the *new theories*, and so far as Methodist doctrine is concerned *they* are the '*heretics.*' It will be remembered that Dr. Poolkins claimed that Mr. Wesley rejected the residue theory in the year 1784, but the paragraph just read is taken from a sermon preached in 1790.

"It will be quite proper before Dr. Poolkins' character passes at the Annual Conference this fall, to find out in some way if he knew that his statements when made were so far out of harmony with the facts.

"I will also read you a few selections from Wesley's Journals, written by him after the time at which Dr. Poolkins tells us Mr. Wesley changed his views:

"'Several of our friends declared that God had saved from inbred sin, with such exactness both of sentiment and language, as clearly showed they were taught of God.' Journal, 1785.

"In May of the same year, we find in Mr. Wesley's Journal this statement: 'Many children, chiefly girls, were indisputably justified; some of them were likewise sanctified, and were patterns of all holiness.'

"To F. Garretson in the same year, he writes:

"'The more explicitly and strongly you press all believers to aspire after full salvation, full sanctification, as attainable now by simple faith, the more the whole work of God will prosper.'

"I could read to this audience many more selections from Wesley's writings, showing clearly his position on the subject, but it is entirely unnecessary.

"In passing, I ask you this simple question: Is it right for an opponent of sanctification, as a second work of grace, to misrepresent Mr. Wesley, in order to deceive Methodist people who are not posted on the subject, and prejudice them against what these men are pleased to call 'second blessingism?'

"I appeal to the Zinzendorfian wing of our Methodist family, Is it, ' *honor bright,*' for you and your leaders thus to undertake to misrepresent the dead, and the plain facts of history, that you may, in a measure, destroy the influence of this great Methodist doctrine, among Methodist people?

"Can you continue to indulge in such willful misrepresentation, and ask us to regard you as honest men? Can you continue to deceive the people with what you well know to be false, and yet retain your self-respect, and confidence in, and respect for each other?

"I demand in the name of common honesty, in the name of a hundred thousand Southern Methodist people, who have read within the last few years the doctrine and history of Methodism, and in the name of our great Judge, who has declared that ' all liars shall have their part in the lake that burneth with fire and brimstone,' that those who oppose the doctrine of the second work of grace, cease slandering

John Wesley, by saying that he did not teach this doctrine, or that he ever changed his views on the subject. [Applause].

" Adam Clarke was one of the most devout Methodists, as well as one of the most profound scholars, of his time. I will give you one paragraph from his comment on John's first epistle, to show you that Clarke was in perfect harmony with Mr. Wesley on this all-important subject, to show you also, that those Methodist preachers who are to be driven from our pulpits as heretics, are in harmony with these great men of God who planted Methodism in the world.

" I will read to you a part of Clarke's comment on the 9th verse of the first chapter of I. John, giving you the inspired word also:

" 'If we confess our sins, he is faithful and just to forgive us our sins, and to cleanse us from all unrighteousness.'

" 'Observe here,' says Clarke: 'I. Sin exists in the soul after two modes, as follows: (1) In guilt, which required forgiveness or pardon. (2) In pollution, which requires cleansing.

" 'II. Guilt, to be forgiven, must be confessed; and pollution, to be cleansed, must be also confessed. In order to find mercy, a man must know and feel himself to be a sinner, that he may fervently apply to God for pardon: in order to get a clean heart, a man must know and feel its depravity, acknowledge and deplore it before God, in order to be fully sanctified.'

"The audience will readily see that these two great Methodists, renowned alike for piety, fruitfulness and scholarship, were what these modern persecutors of their spiritual sons, would call 'second blessingists,' and propose to drive from our pulpits and church as heretics. I stand here to-night to say that these men who have thus assailed the doctrines of their church, and their brethren who believe and teach them, are unworthy of a place in Methodist pulpits, unworthy of the confidence of Methodist people, and unfit to instruct the rising generation of Methodist children. (Applause).

"Richard Watson was one of the most scholarly and pious men, as well as one of the clearest and most forceful writers ever produced by Methodism. His 'Theological Institutes,' contain a statement of Bible doctrine not to be surpassed for clearness and force by any English pen. The volume from which I read is in the Course of Study for our young preach‧ ers. I read from Vol. 2, Part II, page 450:

"'We have already spoken of justification, adop‧ tion, regeneration, and the witness of the Holy Spirit, and we proceed to another as *distinctly marked,* and as *graciously promised* in the Holy Scriptures: this is the *entire sanctification,* or the perfect:d *holi‧ ness* of *believers.*'

"What have we here from this distinguished Methodist writer? What is this *distinctly marked* and *graciously promised* blessing? It is the *entire sanctification* of *believers.* Can it be possible that our College of Bishops recommend the writings of such a ' second blessingist' for the study of our young preachers! If believers in entire sanctification, subsequent to regeneration, are heretics, Richard Watson was a heretic, and our bishops ought not to place the heretical writings of a heretic in the Course of Study for young preachers. I could quote at great length from Watson, but I simply desire to show you that he taught that entire sanctification is different from and subsequent to regeneration.

"William Burt Pope is one of the later writers of English Methodism. His 'Higher Catechism' and his larger treatise on 'Systematic Theology' have received very general endorsement and have been adopted as text-books among the various branches of Methodism throughout the world.

"We will give you a paragraph from Pope's ' What is Meant by *Entire Sanctification?*'

"' This is the work of the Holy Spirit alone, applying the virtue of the atonement in the removal of the last trace of the indwelling or pollution of sin, and consecrating the entire nature of the *believer* to God in perfect love.' Page 256.

"This pollution of indwelling sin is, you see, to

be removed from the *believer's* heart. This one paragraph is amply sufficient to convict Pope of being as guilty of second blessingism as were Wesley, Clarke, and Watson.

"I want now to call your attention to a few plain statements in Methodist history concerning this doctrine. I hold in my hand a book called 'Memorials of Methodism in Virginia.'

"It was written by Rev. William W. Bennett, D.D., and was published in the year 1871.

"Rev. Robert Williams was one of the first men to plant Methodism in Virginia; a friend and co-worker of his was Deveroux Jarratt, a pious clergyman of the Episcopal Church, who was the friend and helper of the early Methodists in Virginia.

"On the 64th page of this book I read these words: 'Jarratt draws this picture of his new friend, Rev. Robert Williams': 'He was a plain, artless, indefatigable preacher of the gospel; he was greatly blessed in detecting the hypocrite, razing false foundations, and stirring up believers to press after a present salvation from the remains of sin.'

"On the 94th page of this book we find these words, descriptive of an old-time Methodist revival: 'In rapid succession the members rose and bore testimony to the saving power of the gospel. Some told how the Lord had justified them freely; others, how and when the blood of Jesus had cleansed them from all sin; while others, with strong cries and abundant tears, sought for pardon or holiness.' Turning to the following page, I read: 'When the preachers closed up their year's work, the result was glorious. Eighteen hundred had been added to the societies. Many had been sanctified and rejoiced in that perfect love that casteth out all fear.' If you will take up McTyeire's History of Methodism, and turn to page 304, you will find an interesting account of Methodist revivals, then being held in this country, sent to Mr. Wesley, from Mr. Jarratt, through Mr. Rankin. I read only a short paragraph: 'I have seen both men and women, who had long been happy in a sense of God's pardoning love, as much convicted on account of the remains of sin in their hearts, and as much distressed for eternal deliverance from them, as ever I saw any for justification. Their whole cry was,

> "'Oh that I now the rest might know,
>   Believe and enter in!
> Now, Savior, now the power bestow,
>   And let me cease from sin.'

"'And I have been present when they believed that God answered this prayer, and bestowed this blessing upon them.

"'I have conversed with them several times since, and have found them thoroughly devoted to

God. They all testify that they have received the gift instantaneously, and by simple faith.

"'We have sundry witnesses of this perfect love who are above all suspicion.'

"Now, I call your special attention to Bishop McTyeire's comment on this report of Jarratt, the Episcopalian, to Wesley. 'This reads,' says the Bishop, 'as if a Methodist had written it.' Ah, indeed!

"Why did not Bishop McTyeire here begin to scoff, and cry out, 'second blessingism,' 'heretics,' 'put them out of the church,' etc.? For the simple reason that Bishop McTyeire was an honest man of intelligence and piety, and a 'true Methodist.'

"In his 'History of Methodism,' Bishop McTyeire remarks of Bishop Whatcoat, 'Born in 1736; converted, September 3, 1758; sanctified, March 28, 1763.' It seems that this *new heresy* was in vogue as far back as 1763, and Bishop Whatcoat was a second blessingist, who ought to have been turned out of the church for heresy. Bishops Asbury and McKendree would have shared the same fate had our modern opposers have lived in their day and been possessed of the same spirit that characterizes them to-day, for Bishops Asbury and McKendree enjoyed the experience, and preached the doctrine of entire sanctification, as a work of grace received subsequent to regeneration. If any of the glib gentlemen of the rabid opposition to Methodism deny these statements, I am prepared to make them eat their words.

"My friends, I should like to quote at length from Methodist history. I could give you a long list of Methodist preachers, as grand a band of heroes as ever trod the earth; among them would be Jesse Lee, Calvin Wooster, Wilbur Fisk, Stephen Olin, Lovick Pierce, and a host of others, whose names are written in heaven, the fruits of whose ministry remain upon the earth to the present day. These are the men whom modern opposers of the great holiness movement have discovered were unfit for membership in the Methodist Church.

"I must not put down Bishop McTyeire's History of Methodism until I have read you at least two more selections from its pages. Philip Bruce was one of the committee of fourteen appointed to draft a plan for a delegated General Conference, and, with Ezekiel Cooper and Joshua Soule, drew up the constitution under which that body is organized. On page 312 of this book, McTyeire says of him: 'Philip Bruce professed, preached, and exemplified sanctification.'

"William Watters and Philip Gatch were the first native preachers reported in the minutes of American Methodism. Speaking of Watters, he says: 'He was not a great preacher, but closing up a happy and prosperous year he gives the key to his success: 'The most glorious work that ever I beheld was in this circuit, among believers. Scores professed to be sanctified unto the Lord. I could not be satisfied without pressing on Christians this privilege; and indeed, I could not but remark that however able the speaker, if nothing of the sanctification of the spirit was dwelt on, believers appeared not to be satisfied, and that however weak, if they, from the fulness of their hearts, and in faith, exhorted believers to go on to perfection, the word was blessed.'

"Notice, that Bishop McTyeire calls this faith in and use of the doctrine of sanctification '*the key to his success.*'

"Suppose these men of immortal fame were living to-day, what sort of treatment would they receive at the hands of Southern Methodism? They would be forbidden to attend or take part in holiness camp-meetings, and if they did not bow like truckling slaves to the tyrannical mandate, they would have charges trumped up against them and be turned out of the Southern Methodist Church.

"We have at least one bishop who could sit up and chew tobacco and see the thing done with as much *sang-froid* as a fiddling Nero manifested while Rome burned.

"I say to you to-night, it would be as easy for a camel to pass through a needle's eye as for John

Wesley, Adam Clarke, John Fletcher, Richard Watson, Asbury, McKendree, and McTyeire to pass muster before such men as Samuel P. Wright, who think that for Zion's sake all second blessingists ought to be tried for heresy and turned out of the church. Impossible, you say; no sir, it is not; already the work has begun, only the heresy feature has been left out. Violation of law has been the false charge on which God's ministers have been driven from us. And I would like to ask you, which one of our bishops has lifted up his voice against these godless proceedings? Not one.

"Show me a word from the pen of E. E. Hoss or Zepheniah Meek, editors of the *Christian Advocate* and *Central Methodist*, in defense of the rights of the true followers of Wesley. It can not be found. The time has come when laymen must awake and hasten to the rescue.

"I will call your attention to two paragraphs in our Book of Discipline. One of them is read when members are received into the church, the other, when preachers are received into the conference.

"On the reception of members into the church, the pastor says, 'Brethren, I commend to your love and care these persons whom we this day recognize as members of the Church of Christ. Do all in your power to increase their faith, confirm their hope, and *perfect them in love.*'

"On receiving preachers into full connection into our conferences, the bishop asks the following questions: 'Have you faith in Christ? Are you going on to perfection? Do you expect to be made perfect in love in this life? Are you groaning after it?' To all of these questions the preachers in the Southern Methodist Church have answered in the affirmative.

"The enemies of truth and righteousness may try to distort the meaning of these two paragraphs all they will, nevertheless the meaning is plain and easy of comprehension.

"It is simply this, the church is exhorted to do all in her power to bring her members into the experience of *perfect love*—entire sanctification, and preachers on reception into the conferences pledge themselves to loyalty to the doctrine by declaring that they are groaning after the experience and expect to obtain it in this life.

"I will close with one verse from one of Charles Wesley's hymns. It is hymn No. 542, in a Methodist hymn book published in Nashville, Tenn., for the M. E. Church, South, in the year 1868:

> "'Speak the second time, 'be clean,'
> Take away my inbred sin;
> Every stumbling block remove;
> Cast it out by perfect love.'

"Here, as a lawyer would say, I rest my case. The subject is not exhausted—it is inexhaustible.

But, for the present, I leave you to think and talk over what I have said. You can but be aware of the fact, that as Methodist people we have been greatly wronged.

"It is clear to my mind that the neglect of this great doctrine by our preachers accounts largely for the great want of spirituality in our church, and the flood of worldliness which has flowed in upon us. The few holiness people among us are like Gideon's faithful band of three hundred who had the courage to break their pitchers, sound their trumpets, and let their lights shine to the confusion and rout of the enemies of Israel."

When Mr. Huton took his seat, the lawyers and city officials hastened to shake his hand, and Judge Hardee arose and said he felt that a vote of thanks was due Mr. Huton for the manner in which he had defended the faith once delivered to the Methodists. It was not his purpose to prove the doctrine script-ural, that had been abundantly proven more than a century ago, but he came here to-night to defend this doctrine against the attacks of unfaithful men, who have crept in among us, and now propose to drive our humble and faithful ministers from our church. "For my part," said Judge Hardee, "I most sincerely thank him for his utterances. I shall make the sub-ject a careful study myself; not that I am not fully convinced, but because of the spiritual benefit I shall derive from such reading. I believe the time has come for laymen to take an active part in these discussions, and to arise as one man to curb and put down the utter disregard of doctrine and law that is manifesting itself among the opposers of the great holiness revival. Let all who join me in a vote of thanks to Brother Huton, stand on their feet."

In a moment every person in the building arose, except one lone person seated in a chair in the aisle, and that person was old Sister Dishrattler. Somehow this sister had learned that the holiness people were opposed to church festivals, and for this reason, if for no other, she would have bitterly opposed the holiness movement.

The congregation was dismissed at once, and as they passed out of the hall, Hicks said, "Huton, come to the office early in the morning, I want to have a talk with you before business hours."

CHAPTER VI.

AN OLD-TIME REVIVAL NEEDED.

The morning following the address delivered at the City Hall, Huton and Hicks, according to promise, met in their law office quite early, when the following conversation took place:

HICKS: "While you were speaking last night a matter was suggested to my mind, and so impressed upon me that I determined to mention it to you. That is why I asked you to meet me here before business hours. This city needs an old-time revival of religion.

HUTON: "There can be no doubt of that fact. I have been thinking and praying about it ever since my conversion the other night. But how to get someone to hold such a meeting for us is the question."

HICKS: "We can hold it ourselves."

HUTON: "I had not thought of that."

HICKS: "Well, sir, with God's help we can do it. It occurred to me last night while you were speaking, that if you could read Wesley's sermons to the people, putting in a comment here and there, followed with exhortation and invitation, we might see a great awakening here. I really believe the people are hungry for a revival. It is something they have not seen here in years. It does not cost us less than six or seven thousand dollars a year to run our church, and if there has been a genuine regeneration in it in the past five years, I have not heard of it."

HUTON: "Think of it, not less than $35,000 invested, and not a soul saved."

HICKS: "Some of our preachers are going to have to face some awful facts in the day of judgment. They have opposed evangelists, ridiculed the holiness movement, and trifled away their time, much of it with cigars stuck in their mouths, while worldliness has flooded the church, and the people have gone to perdition in droves. There is almost no such thing as the fear of God before the eyes of the people of this city."

HUTON: "Well, it is plain enough to me, that the anti-holiness preachers will never arouse the conscience of a community by inveighing against 'second blessingism.'"

HICKS: "There is not a doubt in my mind that if our bishops, presiding elders, pastors and local preachers had fallen into line twenty years ago, when the holiness movement first began to make headway in the South, rallied around the old Methodist doctrine of entire sanctification, subsequent to regeneration, we would to-day have one of the most united and powerful evangelistic bodies of Christians in the world."

HUTON: "Yes, and would now throughout tne South and West be in the midst of one of the most powerful revivals of religion in the world's history."

HICKS: "There is a fearful responsibility resting upon those men in our church who have forsaken our doctrines, and opposed them, and while they have claimed to be the truly loyal, have walked roughshod over the law, in order to drive from our church the loyal sons of Wesley, and of God."

HUTON: "Yes, they get up a sort of a mock trial, turn a layman out for assisting at a camp-meeting, or a local preacher for proclaiming the gospel of full salvation to the poor people out in the woods somewhere, and then call them the *disgruntled.*"

HICKS: "Not only have they turned them out of the church for no other crime than that of getting sinners converted and believers sanctified, but they have followed them into other churches with misrepresentation and ridicule, and have become angry and bitter against any other denomination that has given them a home, the communion of the Lord's Supper while they live, and Christian burial when they die."

HUTON: "Which one of these leaders of anti-Wesleyan theories has proven a blessing to the church, or community in which he has ministered, or lived? Who, of all of them, will be remembered as a man of deep piety, great spiritual power, and

as a fearless hero against the present sinful generation in which we are living? Name me one of them,
Hicks, who has written books, newspaper articles, or
preached sermons against this doctrine of entire
sanctification, as a second work of grace, as taught
by Wesley in our standards and history, and by the
present holiness movement, who has put great force
and power into the Methodism of these times, that
will be felt in the cause of salvation ten years, or
six months as to that matter, after he is gone."

HICKS: "I cannot point out the man you ask for.
I have taken the church paper, read the new books
written by the anti-Wesleyans; in fact, have kept up
with the holiness movement, and the opposition to
it, in all of its phases, and the man you mention is
not among all of them. There are many attractive
men, a whole host of little doctors of divinity, some
good, popular speakers, and quite a number of them
in position in the church who are the avowed enemies of this doctrine, but there is not one of them
who is a great intellectual, moral or spiritual force
in his day and generation. There are many good and
useful men in our church who are not entirely orthodox, from a Wesleyan point of view, for whom I
have no word of complaint or censure. I am speaking of the avowed enemies of this great Methodist
doctrine."

HUTON: "Say, Hicks, it seems you have kept up

with these things pretty well, why have you never sought the experience?"

HICKS: ;"I have, but somehow I have never gone at it with the earnestness that should have characterized my seeking. I believe I have been very near the blessing several times, but somehow it seemed to slip away from me. My consecration has never been just what it should have been, I suppose, and the matter was not as definite in my mind as it should have been. I begin to understand it now far more clearly than ever before."

HUTON: "My mind is fully made up on a few points: (1) It is a Bible truth. Of this fact I have not the shadow of a doubt; (2) It is for all of God's children. Of this I feel perfectly sure; (3) I intend to seek for it with all my heart, and the Bible is full of promises to me: I cannot open the book and not find them. I find it in almost every chapter."

HICKS: "Well, that is the way to go at it, here is my hand as a pledge that I too will seek with all my heart this full salvation."

The men clasped hands, and for some seconds sat in silence. Each one of them turned to his desk with moistened eyes.

Dr. Poolkins had written to his Presiding Elder telling him of his wife's bad health, and asking him, if possible, to supply the pulpit until Conference.

The elder had secured a theological student at

Vanderbilt who came to remain to the close of the Conference year. He preached to a large and serious congregation on the Sabbath, both morning and evening, and left Monday to attend the commencement exercises, and then to return and take charge of the church.

The news of the whole matter of Dr. Poolkins' sermons on the holiness craze, his challenge to all comers, Huton's acceptance of it, and Mrs. Poolkins' sudden decline in health, soon spread through all the country, and through the Annual Conference, of which Dr. Poolkins' charge was one of the most important appointments.

The matter was discussed generally, and the general impression was, that the Doctor would not return to his charge, but would put in his time looking after his wife's health, and then by some means get a transfer to some Southern or Western Conference.

The following conversation was heard between two Methodist preachers on the train one day, about two weeks after Poolkins left the city of Newton. The two men referred to were among the most prominent in their Conference. I think it is wise to withhold their names. This will be apparent to the reader as he proceeds.

Rev. Mr. A was a man well advanced in years, and withal a substantial man, a leader in his Conference, devoted to his church, and well capable of filling any pulpit in the Conference to which he belonged.

Rev. Mr. B was a younger man, but a man of considerable experience and fine ability. Rev. Mr. A sat down by B on the train, the compliments of the day were exchanged, and after each one had given to the other some account of his charge, Mr. A said: "Of course you have heard of the Poolkins' episode."

B: "Yes, my judgment is that we will see him in these parts no more, and for my part I must say that my opinion is, that the loss of the people he goes to, will be our gain."

A: "This is a new way of putting it, but I am not sure that it is not the correct way. Poolkins has been here in our Conference four years, has had two of our best appointments, and if he has been of any sort of advantage to Methodism in this State in any way, I have not heard of it."

B: "Do you know, I have a real curiosity to know why it is that the Bishops take up a man like Poolkins and transfer him from one Conference to another and put him down in our best appointments? Poolkins is one of a number of his class who have been flying from Conference to Conference for the past fifteen years and getting the very best, and if they have done anything that has been of real service to the church, I do not know anything of it. We have had three or four of them in the last few years, and they have been a real disadvantage to us."

A: "No doubt of that, my brother. Take these men who have been among us, of whom you speak, not one of them has been a scholar or a man of deep piety, or a revivalist, or a solid, sound, every day preacher. The churches have not developed spiritually or financially under their spread-eagle ministry, and one of the evils of their coming among us is, that the churches served by them have a notion that they must have transfers from this time on. They think they are of an intellectual caliber above the preachers in our Conference, and we easily have thirty men among us the superiors of the transfers who have been sent in."

B: "Yes, we built up the appointments, erected the churches, built and furnished the parsonages, and then had to step down and out for transfers. I am not so much objecting to transfers, but the class of men that have been sent in on us.

"If we are to get an idea of the Bishop's estimate of our ability by our last three or four transfers, we are forced to the conclusion that they place a low estimate upon us. I must say I have been deeply chagrined by their sending in about second or third rate men to fill our first-class appointments.

It is a disadvantage to us every way. It discour-
ages our young and rising men. 'It is equivalent
to the Bishop and the Church telling them that they
are unfit to man a first-class appointment, and we
have men among us to-day who have been dwarfed
in their intellectual growth by being kept in the
background. Take George E. Tarlton for an example. George is a man of liberal education, fine
personal appearance, and good natural endowments,
and a splendid preacher of Bible truth, but he has
been kept back in the country towns that our transfers might have our city appointments, and the con-
sequence is he has not gotten out into the current of
things, and has not the breadth and grasp he would
have had if he could have been placed, at least eight
years ago, in a station that would have called out
all of his power, and made him do his level best.
You see, churches should build up and develop
preachers, as well as preachers build up churches. I
can name a dozen young men in our Conference,
who could be developed into pastors and preachers
of a very high order, if we can give them appointments that will put them on their mettle, and bring
them in contact with the thinking, aggressive men
of the Church.

"They are being wronged, kept back, stultified,
and the truth is more or less prejudiced against our
bishops, because of the transfer of ordinary men,

who are evidently place-hunters, into our Conference, to occupy the places that we could so easily
fill, and ought to fill with our own men.

"It would be very unfortunate for our preachers
and people to come to feel that there was an injudi-
cious and unholy favoritism on the part of any of
our bishops, that would lead them to seek good places
for second-rate men, regardless of the best interests
of the church and conferences."

A: "Quite true, and yet that impression is getting among our preachers. You see, when a man is
sent in on us, without our wish or consent, with a
flourish of trumpets, and directly it begins to leak
out that he is inexcusably in debt, and worst of all,
will not tell the truth to his creditors; or that once
or twice his character has been arrested on charges
of the gravest nature involving his moral character;
or that he is a habitual and well-known plagiarist,
or that he has been frequently drunk in some other
conference, the preachers will at once begin to
inquire, did the bishop who placed him in our conference, and in our best charge, know his record?
If he did not, he ought to have known it, for it is
well known. If the bishop knew his record, how
could he consistently place him in our midst, and over
us, in a sense, by giving him our best station?

"From my own personal knowledge this State has
had all the characters described above, transferred

in on us within the past dozen years. True, they were birds of passage, and did not stay long, but they did us harm in more ways than one. They spoiled several very good stations, which having had transfers, are not now willing to be supplied by our conference men. Our preachers are disgusted with the whole procedure, they feel that it is unjust, and that God's hand is not in it at all. It has damaged the influence of our bishops almost irreparably; and, worst of all, those same unworthy men are somewhere in our connection to-day, doing for some other conference just what they have done for us. I should not be surprised if this sort of thing would result in a limitation of the appointing power now vested in our chief pastors."

B: " Well, the evil is a growing one, a serious one, and at no distant day must have a remedy, or the church will suffer great loss."

A: "Of course I would not for a moment intimate that all transfers are worthless men. Some of the best and most useful men in our church are transfers, and yet I have an idea that they, and the church at large would be better off if they should settle down in some conference, and remain there. To my mind the transfer question is to-day a more serious and important question than the evangelist question. But here is my station; good-bye, Brother B."

No doubt the reader is beginning to wonder what has become of Dr. Poolkins and his sick wife. It will suffice for the present to say that Mrs. Bishop Helper gave them a most hearty welcome. She was much surprised that the Doctor had left his important charge to come with his wife, but more surprised to find that Sister Poolkins was looking so remarkably well. She had a letter half finished to the Bishop when they arrived; in the latter half of it she told of the coming of the preacher and his wife, also assured the Bishop that all the good woman needed was a few weeks' rest. The Bishop replied to the letter at once. His letter reached his wife the ninth day after the coming of her visitors. She read the following paragraph to the Doctor:

"I was glad to learn from your letter that Sister Poolkins is in a much better state of health than we had suspected. No doubt she will soon be fully herself again. Give Bro. Poolkins my kindest regards, and say to him, if he has not gone already, that my advice is that he hasten back to his charge at once, and remain there until conference. There was some objection to his being stationed there. I made the appointment, and I am concerned both for the church and for him. Tell him not to delay his return to his work."

The poor doctor dropped his head when the letter was read to him. The Bishop's wife, and Mrs. Poolkins urged him to leave on the first train the following day, that he might fill his pulpit the next Sabbath.

Dr. Poolkins excused himself and went to his room, the good women supposed, to pack his trunk for the homeward journey, but they were mistaken. He sat in deep thought for some time, and then his face lit up with a happy thought, and he seized his pen and wrote the following letter, of which he made twenty copies, and mailed to that number of preachers in the county towns scattered about in the State in which, for the present, he was a refugee from the justice Huton was so ready to mete out to him:

"*Dear Brother:* For the present I am in your State with my dear wife, for the benefit of her health. While her condition is not such that my presence with her all the time is necessary, at the same time I am unwilling to leave her and return to my pastorate some hundreds of miles away in another State.

"I write to say to you that I have an excellent lecture which I believe will entertain, amuse and edify any audience. If the young people of your church will make a date with me, make arrangements, advertise, etc., I will deliver the lecture for one-half of the door receipts. Please look after the matter and write me at once, that I may keep open a date for you. Address me at New Orleans, La. My subject is 'Love, Courtship and Marriage.'"

The following morning at breakfast he informed the ladies that he had to run down to New Orleans to look after some matters, his twenty letters were promptly mailed, and he left for the city on the nine o'clock train.

CHAPTER VII.

THE REV. MR. YOUNGDUCK.

Dr. Poolkins spent a few days in New Orleans writing to the pastors of small stations, offering to arrange with the Epworth Leagues, to deliver his lecture on "Love, Courtship and Marriage," for one half of the cash receipts, and visiting the post-office many times a day.

Soon the seed which he had sown began to produce a harvest, and little pastors in every quarter who were striving hard to interest and hold together their little Epworth Leagues, often spending more time and patience on the twenty-five or thirty members in their churches, who constituted that society, than with all the rest of their two to four hundred members, were eagerly writing the dear doctor to make them a date as soon as possible.

Many a town and village was thrown into a flutter of excitement over the coming of the great Dr. Poolkins to deliver his celebrated lecture on "Love, Courtship and Marriage." The zealous and truly loyal were really thankful to have some church work to do, and at various points of the compass, old maids, bewitching young ladies, and little girls were on the streets, in the stores and shops — some of them mustering up courage to approach dignified bankers — selling tickets to the lecture, and gathering in the precious quarters for the church. Could you have seen the busy-bee appearance of things about the parsonages and churches of some of the little towns, where the Epworth Leaguers had entered into the real spirit of the enterprise, you would have thought that the long-promised "wave of prosperity" had come at last. It would be interesting if we had the time to follow Dr. Poolkins on his first lecture tour. He was the guest of honor in many parsonages, often comfortably quartered in the elegant home of some judge or leading lawyer, where the dear sisters listened with mingled awe and admiration while the doctor told of the wonderful feats he had performed as pastor of large city churches.

Dr. Poolkins' long, graceful coat skirts and shining plug hat made a fine impression as he hurried through the main street of the small towns and large villages, and more than one boy looked after him with the ambitious hope that he might be a great city pastor some day, in straight-breasted coat, with skirts coming below his knees, and shiny beaver plug on his head, and a popular lecturer, going from place to place, delivering speeches to Epworth Leagues.

It never occurred to them that the plug hat worn by our doctor was not full of brains to the top, while the truth is one might have shot through the hat with a 44-caliber Winchester more than half way down from the top and not have endangered its wearer in the least.

Thus Dr. Poolkins spent the precious weeks, while lost multitudes of his fellow-beings all about him were rushing unprepared into eternity.

How a man with the call of God to preach the Gospel, ringing in his soul, can reconcile himself to come down from the pulpit to the lecture platform to entertain and amuse the people, we can not understand.

The lecture platform is a good institution, doubtless, but it is not the place for the minister of the gospel; yet in these latter days it has been Satan's method of seducing many heralds of the cross.

They have turned aside from the high calling of warning men from the pulpit, to seek the applause of men on the platform, and of them in the end it might be written, as it was written of Samson, "he wist not that the Lord had departed from him."

Only a few days had passed since the conversation between Hicks and Huton with reference to an effort for a revival in their city, when they, after more fully maturing their plans, determined to call on their young pastor, who was supplying the pulpit until conference, and lay the matter before him. They found him in the church study busily engaged in the preparation of his Sabbath sermon.

They explained to him in a few words that they were anxious for a revival of religion in their church and city, and would be glad to have his co-operation in the proposed effort.

The Rev. Mr. Youngduck (which was the pastor's name) said he hardly thought it the proper season of the year for a revival effort.

"Well, Bro. Youngduck," said Hicks, "it may not be the best time for a meeting, but for some years we have had pastors who have objected to revival meetings, and it is entirely possible that we may have another of the same sort sent to us by the next conference, so we thought it would be well to try and have our meeting now, lest we should get some man who will not want a meeting at all."

"You see," said Huton, "Bro. Hicks and myself both have children who are unsaved, and we are intensely interested in the matter."

MR. YOUNGDUCK: "Are either of you a licensed preacher?"

HUTON: "No, brother, but our hearts are drawn out for the lost souls in our homes and community, and we are anxious to do something, if possible, to awaken the people and bring them to repentance."

HICKS: "All we ask, Bro. Youngduck, is the use of the basement of the church, and if you do not wish to co-operate with us, we will call on God for help, and do what we can for the salvation of the lost. We believe the people are deeply interested, and greatly desire just such a meeting as we propose to hold. Mr. Huton will be our leader; he will read one of Wesley's sermons, comment on it, close with an exhortation, and we believe souls will be saved."

HUTON: "You see, brother, I was a church member in good standing for many years, but an unsaved man, and reading 'Wesley's Sermons' brought me to a sense of my condition, and to Christ. Our people have no idea of the powerful truths contained in these neglected volumes, and we believe if we can read these sermons to them, there will be no small stir among them. All we ask is the use of the basement-room in our church."

YOUNGDUCK: "Well, I will see about it, and give you an answer in a few days."

Our two laymen were a little surprised that there should be any hesitancy in letting them have the basement of the church for a meeting, but determined to await results patiently, and left the chuch with the promise of an early answer.

Rev. Mr. Youngduck at once wrote the following letter to his presiding elder:

"REV. JOSEPHUS S. GALL, D. D.,

"*Dear Brother:* I wish you could come over and spend a few days with us, and help steer the old ship clear of some dangerous rocks.

"I find a couple of lawyers here who seem to

want to run things. They are the fellows who were the cause of all the trouble with Poolkins. They want to hold a meeting in the basement of our church, and propose to read 'Wesley's Sermons,' or something of that kind. I think it is an effort to run the second blessingism craze in on us. The thing ought to be nipped in the bud.

"I want you to write to me at once, saying that they can not have the church building for any such meetings. It seems to me that there are some laymen in the country who are becoming entirely too officious. If you want to keep the holiness movement plague out of this congregation, you must act at once, and with a positive decision that will be felt. Yours fraternally,

"FREDERIC CLARK HARRIS YOUNGDUCK."

To this letter there came a reply in a few days which read as follows:

"REV. FREDERIC CLARK HARRIS YOUNGDUCK,

"*My Very Dear Brother:* Your letter came promptly to hand. Let me commend your wisdom and jealous care for the welfare of our beloved Zion, and thank you for writing to me about these matters which so deeply concern every truly loyal son and daughter of Southern Methodism.

"Please say to those brethren that I positively refuse to permit our church to be used for any meeting on eccentric lines.

"I understand that these same disturbers of our peace have on foot a scheme looking toward the establishment of a holiness camp-meeting. You will do me a great favor if you will find out the facts with regard to the matter, and write me accordingly. Like yourself, I think these things should be nipped in the bud. Yours faithfully,

"JOSEPHUS S. GALL, D. D."

The young supply read Dr. Gall's letter with great pleasure, and at once dropped a note to the two lawyers, informing them that they could not use the basement of the church for the proposed meetings.

On the same evening that Mr. Youngduck sent his note to the lawyers, Huton received a letter signed by some twenty-five leading men of the city, which read as follows:

"HON. GEORGE M. HUTON,

"*Dear Sir:* It was our pleasure to hear you a few evenings since at the City Hall deliver an address setting forth the doctrines of your church on entire sanctification.

"As you are perhaps aware, there has been much talk on the subjcet, and we, the undersigned, are anxious to have you deliver a second address in the City Hall, in which you will treat the subject from a Bible standpoint.

"We beg leave to suggest that you take for your theme, 'Entire Sanctification a Second Work of Grace, as Taught in the Scriptures.' You get our idea, we leave the wording to you. Hoping to hear favorably, etc.

"P. S.—We wish to say if you consent to deliver the address, we will arrange the hall, advertise, and insure you a large and appreciative audience."

Huton took this note to his friend Hicks, who urged him to accept the invitation at once.

"Well, Hicks," said Huton, "I hardly like to undertake that. I am not well posted on the subject from a Bible standpoint; besides, I do not like to make a talk on that line when I have not got the experience myself."

HICKS: "These men simply want you to show them the Scriptures out of which Methodists get their authority for their views on the subject. The subject is agitated, let's keep it going. It will be a good advertisement for our camp-meeting, and can but do good."

Huton wrote a note to the parties, accepting their invitation, and fixing the date for Friday evening, June 15th, twenty days off, that he might have ample time to make preparation.

Bro. Youngduck and Sister Dishrattler were noticed driving about the city together most all of the latter part of the week, all of which was explained on the Sabbath morning when Mr. Youngduck announced that on Friday evening, June 15th, the Young People's Missionary Society would give a cake-walk in the basement of the church, after which refreshments would be served. There would be an admission fee of fifteen cents, the proceeds would be devoted to the cause of missions. The reader will notice that Huton's lecture on Sanctification and the cake-walk were appointed for the same evening. Meanwhile our two lawyers arranged to hold their protracted services in a large, empty store. The building was rented for three months, cleaned and freshly papered, well seated, a platform erected, and an ample altar-rail for penitents arranged.

Their purpose was to announce their meetings at this City Hall meeting, on the evening of June 15th, and go forward and hold afternoon prayer-meetings, and at night Huton was to read and comment on "Wesley's Sermons."

CHAPTER VIII.

CONTUMACIOUS CONDUCT.

Mr. Youngduck learned the purpose of the lawyers and wrote to Dr. Gall to come at once to the scene of action.

Dr. Gall was soon in the city, and sent for our lawyers to meet him in the pastor's study for conference. Hicks and Huton were there at the appointed hour, when the following conversation took place:

DR. GALL: "I understand you brethren propose to hold a second-blessing meeting in an old store."

HICKS: "Well, yes; I suppose that is what you would call it. We propose to hold a meeting, and our desire and aim shall be the conversion of sinners and the sanctification of believers."

DR. GALL: "Well, brethren, it becomes my painful duty to enter my positive protest against your holding this meeting. It can but make trouble in the church. It is a flagrant violation of the law, and you can not afford to be disloyal to your church vows. You know when you were taken into the church you promised obedience to those in authority."

HUTON: "Do I understand you to say that our church vows give you authority to forbid our holding meetings in the store, when such meetings are held.

not for any sort of organization, but simply for the salvation of souls?"

DR. GALL: "Yes; all the services held in the bounds of my district are under my control, and you have no right to hold these meetings over my protest, and if you persist in doing so, much as it will pain me, I shall be compelled to institute proceedings against you for contumacious conduct. I am fully determined that the law of the church shall be respected in my district."

HUTON: "Dr. Gall, Brother Hicks and myself are official members in our church here, and have been for many years; we have both been liberal contributors to the support of the church, and desire to continue loyal and true. But we both have grown children, who have grown up in the church, who are unsaved, and we are deeply concerned for them. We have many friends and acquaintances in this city who are unsaved, and our one object in holding these meetings is the salvation of our families and neighbors. We will attend the services of our church, and not pay a nickle less into its coffers on account of these meetings. All we want is the salvation of souls."

DR. GALL: "I propose that no meetings shall be held in this district without my approval and consent, and I object to your proposed meetings They must not be held."

HICKS: "But, doctor, we will in no way interfere with the regular services of our church. We will seek only the salvation of souls. We will not organize, or do anything that can in any way hinder the work of our church, and, as we believe God is leading us in this matter, we will most certainly hold the meetings."

DR. GALL: "To do so will be a flagrant violation of your church vows, and I will most certainly try and expel you both from the Methodist Church."

HUTON: "Well, doctor, suppose we should conclude to give up the idea of the meetings in the store, and I should fix up an arbor in my back yard on the alley there, and hold the meetings in my yard; or suppose I hold them in my double parlors. Have you any objection to that?'

DR. GALL: "That is the merest dodge. What difference would that make in the matter? Of course I object."

HICKS: "But, doctor, we have unsaved children and unsaved neighbors, and all in the world we desire is their salvation, and we feel that we can not sit still and be guiltless."

DR. GALL: "The church is the place to hold meetings; let them come to the church and be saved."

HUTON: "People do not get saved in our church. There has not been a genuine regeneration in our church in years, and we do not feel that we can remain inactive in matters of such vast importance. Besides, the church has been refused us for these meetings."

DR. GALL: "Well, it is their own fault if the people are not saved. If people will not come to church and seek salvation they deserve to be lost."

HUTON: "I must confess I do not like such statements, and I undertake to say the fault is not with the people. If you ministers had the old-time power that characterized the ministry of the early Methodist preachers, things would be different. Now, doctor, here are the simple facts. Our families and our neighbors are unsaved; there has not been a soul saved in our church for years, and there is not the slightest indication that such a thing will occur, and I must say that those of you who have had charge for some years now do not seem to me to feel any special concern on that line. Now we propose to hold a few services in an old store, seeking to save the lost, and you threaten to turn us out of the church. You will not permit us to hold meetings for the salvation of souls even in our own yard. Worse still, you enter your protest against such meetings in my own parlor. Now, let me tell you, Doctor Gall, I for one will never submit to such tyranny, and I will not leave my church, or be turned out of it either. There is no holier cause than that of religious liberty, and I will no more surrender this God-given right to you than I would surrender it to the Pope at Rome."

DR. GALL: "Very well, sir, do your worst. The bishops of our church, and the authorities at Nashville, will stand back of me, and I intend to enforce the law at any cost."

HUTON: "Yes; I fully understand that there are a lot of petty tyrants in our church, encouraged in their little work by men in high places, but we will appeal our case to the people, and the time is not far distant when your high-handed methods will work your downfall, and forever destroy the prestige and influence of those who sympathize with you and encourage you in your persecutions against the Church of Christ. We deeply regret any trouble that may arise, but our minds are made up."

"Then you will have to take the consequences," said Dr. Gall, and he and Mr. Youngduck, bidding the lawyers good morning, arose and left the room.

Dr. Gall was a typical holiness fighter, literally soaked and saturated with tobacco juice. He had told anecdotes and vulgar jokes and preached the same old sermons on the Darwinian theory, and a few other musty, impractical subjects, over his present district for more than three years. If a soul had been saved under his ministry in fifteen years, no one knew of it. He was of no more real value to the church than a last year's cornstalk is to a farmer. And yet he was one of the many who in the last few years have been put forward to lord it over God's heritage, talk loyalty, and drive God's people out of the Southern Methodist Church.

When the news of Dr. Gall's objections to the meetings in the store was spread through the city the people were indignant, and many who had thought but little of the meetings determined to attend.

Friday afternoon of June the 8th, Huton left the city for a few days' visit to a sister of his who lived only a short distance up the river. He said to Hicks, who walked with him to the boat: "I will not be back until Friday afternoon; you see that things are in proper shape at the City Hall. I want to go out in the country where my mind will be free from either care or disturbance, so that I may study this subject without distraction. More than that, I hope to come back to the city a sanctified man."

CHAPTER IX.

ENTERING CANAAN.

Fortunately for Huton, when he arrived at his sister's home in the country, he found boarding with her the teacher of the district school, Miss Grace Lovell, a woman of culture and fine intelligence, who had for many years been in the enjoyment of the experience of entire sanctification.

This school teacher had watched with interest the part that Huton had taken in defense of the doctrines of the church, and had been deeply concerned about his personal experience. Under her instructions, Huton devoted himself to searching the Scriptures and seeking for the blessing of full salvation.

Having believed in it even before his conversion, and having been a seeker for the blessing from the very day of his regeneration, he did not have to cross at the swellings of the Jordan, but he entered in at Kadesh Barnea, not without a struggle, however. His conflict came with reference to preaching the Gospel. It seemed that all else was on the altar, but somehow he found it very difficult to consent to spend the remainder of his days a minister of the Gospel of Christ. In fact, he could not positively make up his mind that he was Divinely called to

preach. Miss Lovell advised him to place that matter on the altar also, with a complete surrender of
his will to preach, or not to preach, as the Lord
should lead—simply to submit himself to the will of
God in that and all other matters.

Mr. Huton had always stood well in his city,
indeed, throughout the State. Wherever he was
known—and he was quite largely known—he was
regarded as a man of excellent balance, and unusual
common sense.

He found within himself a desire to maintain
his good reputation; he shrank from the thought of
being regarded weak-minded and a crank.

"It seems to me," he said to Miss Lovell, "that I
should be careful to maintain my good reputation.
You see it will enable me to do much more good than
I could otherwise do."

"Your Lord made himself of no reputation,"
said his teacher. "He even suffered the contradic-
tion of sinners against Himself. You must be willing," said she, "to give up the respect of men, and
the personal friendship of your most highly prized
friends, if it should become necessary, in order that
you may have the indwelling Christ in all of His
fulness."

As Huton went forward, led of the Spirit, he
got conceptions of sin he had never had before; the
sins he had committed before his conversion, came

up in memory, and he loathed them with all his heart. He was filled with an awful sense of the uncleanness of his own breast, and found himself repeating the words of Isaiah; "Unclean! Unclean!" He discovered a feeling within his heart closely akin to prejudice against those persons who were opposing the holiness movement, and he found it necessary to humble himself in the very dust before God, in prayer for a perfect deliverance from any sort of prejudice against such persons.

There was one Scripture which the Spirit applied especially to his mind and heart. It is found in John's Gospel, chapter 5, verse 44: "How can ye believe which receive honor one of another?" He saw that one of the greatest obstacles in the way of sanctifying faith in Christ, arises out of a want of a complete abandonment, on the part of the seeker, of all of men's notions, their approval, or even their respect. In a word, to become dead to human honor, to cease to seek it, to go further, and refuse to receive it, to be willing to be led of the Lord, even when to do so meant the loss of reputation for good level-headedness among men who stand high in social, business, and church life.

Not to become a crank, mark you, but to be willing to be thought to be a crank—to be called a crank.

Huton saw in the light of this Scripture the peculiar difficulty under which Methodist preachers,

who would seek the second work of grace, have to
labor. In many instances the whole organization of
the church is against them. We have seen a struggling preacher striving to enter this Canaan, when
the leading laymen of his congregation, his presiding elder, and his bishop, as well as the central
organ of his church, were all against him. He has
loved his church from childhood, the presiding elder
has been looked upon with a reverence and love next
to that given to his father. To him a Methodist
Bishop has always been the greatest of all men,
entirely above the thought of criticism. While he
has been all unconscious of it, he has come to look
upon and feel toward a bishop in his church, almost
as a devout Catholic does toward the Pope at
Rome.

While he would shrink from voting a bishop infal-
lible, he could hardly conceive of one doing a willful
wrong, or making a serious mistake. To criticise or
find fault with a bishop, seems to him to be almost
sacrilegious. As for his church paper, it has, for
years, been second only to his Bible. But now he has
met with some wholly sanctified people, he has
become interested in the subject, he finds the Bible
full of it, he finds the standards and history of his
church full of it, he finds that the old bishops (great
men they were) preached the doctrine and enjoyed
the experience. His own heart is mightily wrought

upon, he is hungering and thirsting after righteousness, and seeking for an entire sanctification from all sin. His presiding elder comes along, preaches against the doctrine, says it is a new heresy, and must be checked or it will split the church! He also takes the young brother aside and warns him not to become a fanatic: "You have fine prospects, and the people want you, there are good openings and calls for you, but if you get mixed up with this holiness movement there will soon be no place that will have you. You have already hurt your influence with some of your best members; now, take a friend's advice, quit reading that PENTECOSTAL HERALD, buckle down to business, and make a man of yourself." All this, and much more. Our brother's mind is disturbed, he hardly knows what to do; he longs to be a useful man, he cannot bear the idea of offending the church he loves, and to displease his presiding elder is simply out of the question.

He goes up to the annual conference. The Bishop's opening speech contains many oblique expressions that are plainly against the holiness people. Through the entire conference, in talks, speeches, and sermons, there runs a sarcastic vein of ridicule of the second blessing, and to our seeker's amazement, the conference smiles and swallows it all down with as much relish as if it were sound sense, and good Methodism.

Horse-racing, theatre going, dancing, card playing church members are highly pleased.　Our seeker
takes a walk and thinks.　He fasts, and remains in his
room and prays.　The Holy Ghost illuminates him,
like the prodigal son in the far country he comes to
himself, he is amazed to find that he has been almost
an idolater, worshiping the church, and those who are
supposed to be great men in it.　He calls mightily
upon Christ to come and cleanse His temple.　He sings:

"The dearest idol I have known,
　　Whate'er that idol be;
　Help me to tear it from Thy throne,
　　And worship only Thee."

He wins the victory.　Christ arises and shines
forth, "the fairest among ten thousand, the One
altogether lovely," and men drop back into the place
in which they belong; he no longer worships or
cowers before them.

There is a marvelous love in his heart for all
good men, whatever their station in life, and a deep
pity for all bad men, even if they are in high and
sacred positions.

He goes forward "free indeed."　Censure and
scorn are heaped upon him, but his whole soul is full
of sacred, holy fire.　Peace reigns within him, he
faces the whole world with a consciousness that God
is with him, and that somehow, though he does not

understand it, "all things" must work together for his good. The man who has reached the point where the one supreme desire of his heart is, not the applause of men, nor their honor, but the honor which God bestows, has won a victory indeed.

Huton won this victory; he put the church and all of its dignitaries and rulers, wife, children, law partner, friends and enemies, all upon the altar of a complete surrender to God. The enemy presented to his mind startling pictures of a future of poverty, humiliation, and disrespect, but he refused to take back aught of the price which he had laid down.

Now he waited, watching his heart, expecting every moment it would bound and throb with hallowed bliss far surpassing anything he had ever known before; and so the hours of watching passed, until finally, at the suggestion of Miss Lovell, he changed his point of view, and, taking his mind's eye from his heart, he fixed and centered his faith on Jesus; all else seemed to fade from view, all else dropped from his mind. Calvary rose before him; never before had he gotten such a conception of the sufferings of his Lord, or the efficiency of His cleansing blood. As he gazed in wonder and in love, he commenced to sing:

> "The half has never yet been told,
> Of love so full and free.
> The half has never yet been told,
> The blood, it cleanseth me."

When this song broke upon the stillness of the night the clock had struck one, but the sister and Miss Lovell, who were in another part of the house, heard in it the note of victory, and they knew that Huton was wholly sanctified. The Spirit bore the unmistakable witness. There could be no doubt.

Huton fell asleep as conscious that he had been wholly sanctified from all sin, instantaneously, subsequent to his regeneration, as he was conscious of his own personal existence

CHAPTER X.

APPEAL TO THE SCRIPTURES.

When Huton awoke the next morning he was so conscious of perfect peace that he seemed to taste peace in his mouth, and the taste of it was like the sweetest honey. And now for the first time he was as fully conscious of a call to preach the Gospel, as he was of the entire sanctification of his soul. He accepted the situation without surprise, murmuring or elation. His consecration had been complete, and now he had no more struggles, but simply cheerful obedience.

On Friday evening Huton returned to the city, arriving just in time to go to the City Hall where an immense throng of people awaited him. As he passed by the Methodist Church he noticed that it was brilliantly lighted up, and decorated for the cake walk which was to take place in the basement of the building.

Mr. Youngduck, and Sister Dishrattler had canvassed the membership of the church thoroughly, and had told the young people especially that they would be *disloyal* if they went to the city hall instead of coming to church, "besides that, just think of the poor heathen," said Sister Dishrattler, "the income of this entertainment will go to the heathen, after expenses are paid." The novelty of the entertainment drew a large crowd, the young people who participated, blacked their faces, and dressed up like colored people, and marched to dance music, with a skip and hop, that very nearly approached a dance. When the cake walk was over, a number of young men employed the Newton string band and adjourned to Sister Dishrattler's with a party of young ladies, all of them Methodists, and went into a long back hall and danced until three o'clock the following morning. And now, oh reader, be not too severe on Sister Dishrattler, for just such things as the above, have occurred in Methodist circles, not far from the spot where I write.

When Huton entered the hall the people were singing. Hicks had offered prayer, and Huton at once went to the speaker's desk on the platform. As he stood there, Bible in hand, the people noted the remarkable change in his face, which was now luminous with the joy of full salvation.

At the close of the song the most perfect silence prevailed and all eyes were fixed on the speaker.

"When I spoke to you in this hall a few weeks since," said Huton, "I prefaced my remarks, by telling you that while preparing my address for you I had been converted. It gives me great pleasure to tell you now that while preparing for the talk of this evening I have been most graciously sanctified. I make all my boast in the Lord. It is all of His infinite goodness and power. He willed it for me, He wrought it in me, He alone can keep me, and shall have all the praise for my full salvation. I have been asked to prove to you from the Scriptures that entire sanctification is a work wrought subsequent to justification, or that the complete cleansing of the heart comes after the forgiveness of sins.

"I beg you in the beginning to remember that I am not a preacher, and do not know how to prepare, and deliver a sermon. But I shall try to read and explain to you some of the Scriptures on the subject the best I can. First of all, there is this that I can most positively affirm. The God revealed in the Bible loves holiness and hates sin, and the devil revealed in the Bible loves sin and hates holiness. The truth of this statement no man can for a moment controvert. In the very nature of things this must be true. And this being true, it is impossible that a child of God should love *sin*, which God hates, and hate *holiness*, which God loves. This being true, stubborn logic forces us to the conclusion that all those persons who oppose holiness, and advocate sin, although they may be in the churches, and some of them high in authority, are not the children of God.

"Our Saviour once said to certain persons: 'Ye are of your father the devil, and the works of your

father ye will do.' Doubtless these words of our
Lord are true. No one in this audience will question the words of Jesus. In the very nature of things
the devil must hate holiness and love sin, hence all
of those who are found opposing holiness, and advo-
cating, or excusing or allowing sin, are of their
father the devil, and they are doing his works. I
grant you that these are plain statements, but I ask
the audience in all candor, are they not logical?
Every honest, intelligent man, be he saint or sinner,
must agree with me that these statements are
true.

"I must speak plainly here to-night, my fellow
beings. The importance of the subject demands the
utmost candor and plainness of statement. Here in
Newton we have been taught to believe holiness
impossible, and sin a necessity. We and our children
have been taught to look with suspicion and contempt upon anyone who claimed or testified to a salvation that saved from all sin, that washed the heart
from all uncleanness in the blood of Jesus.

"Sad to say, but I speak the simple truth when I
say, that in my own church, the Methodist Church,
the church raised up to spread Scriptural holiness
over these lands, the very words 'holiness' or
'sanctification,' are hated and shunned, and it is a
common thing to hear Methodist people say of
sanctification, 'Oh I do not like that word.' This very

sentence has greeted my ears quite frequently of late.

"I stand in my place to-night to say to this audience that in the city of Newton the pulpits have been giving out on this most momentous sub- ject an *uncertain sound*.

"Our children have grown up to hate—what? *Sin?* NO! They have grown up to hate HOLINESS, and to excuse sin on the ground that it is a necessity. It is sad, nevertheless it is true, that the large majority of the church members of this city are not seeking holiness.

"I grant you that there are many theories of holiness or sanctification afloat in the land, but the trouble is they are only *theories*. Some will tell us that we get sanctified when we are penitent sinners before we are converted, some will tell us that we get sanctified at conversion, some tell us that we will gradually grow into the experience, others tell us that we are sanctified at and in death, and still others tell us that it is with purgatorial fires after death that we must be purified from all sin. The trouble with these theories is, they are nonsensical, impractical and un-Scriptural.

"In reading you the Scriptures on the subject let it be understood that I shall use holiness, sanctifica- tion, perfection, perfect love, and the baptism of the Holy Ghost to mean one and the same thing, for it is by the baptism of the Holy Ghost that our hearts are purified, sanctified, made holy, perfected in love, or brought into the state of Christian perfection.

"The necessity for the second work of grace, or the baptism of the Holy Ghost, purifying the heart subsequent to regeneration, arises out of the fact that men are born in a state of natural depravity, that is, corrupt and impure in their moral natures. It is well expressed by David when he says in the fifty-first Psalm, 'Behold I was shapen in iniquity, and in sin did my mother conceive me.' So conscious are men of this fact of evil within them, that it has not been necessary for them to read the Bible to find it out. Where the missionary has never preached, and the Bible has never been read, we will find men deeply and painfully conscious of the natural corruption of their hearts. This corruption of nature leads to transgression of God's law, which makes us guilty; hence, pardon is necessary, and while pardon blots out our transgressions, we also need the cleansing of our natures. The natural depravity of our nature can not be *pardoned*, it must be *cleansed*. *Actual sins* are *pardoned*. Natural *sin,—corruption* must be cleansed away.

"First, God pardons the sinner, second, He cleanses the believer. The fact that uncleanness remains in those who have been pardoned or born of

the Spirit, is clearly taught by the Apostle Paul in
I. Cor. 3: 1-3. I will read it to you, "And I, brethren,
could not speak unto you as unto spiritual, but as
unto carnal, even as unto babes in Christ. I have
fed you with milk, and not with meat; for hitherto
ye were not able to bear it, neither yet now are ye
able. For ye are yet carnal.'

"There is plain Scripture for you. They were
babes in Christ, had been born into the kingdom,
were children of God—their sins forgiven, but they
were *yet carnal*, there was impurity in their natures,
uncleanness in their hearts, that must be cleansed
away before they can have that holiness without
which no man can see the Lord. Gentlemen of the
jury, this Scripture of itself clearly establishes the
doctrine for which I contend. (Laughter). (The
audience will please to pardon me, I am in the habit
of arguing before a jury, I am a lawyer you remember).

"But to proceed, I will call your attention to
another proof text. I read from Romans, seventh
chapter, beginning with the nineteenth verse. 'For
the good that I would I do not: but the evil which I
would not, that I do. Now if I do that I would not,
it is no more I that do it, but sin that dwelleth
in me.'

"I wish to ask the Christians of this audience if
these statements of the Apostle harmonize with

your experience? You are ready to answer me in the affirmative without a moment's hesitation. Since your conversion your purpose and desire has been to do good, you have resolved most positively in your minds that you would not do evil. And yet alas! The good that you intended you failed to do, and the evil that you resolved against you did do. You determined to have a sweet temper, and in a moment found yourself angry. You resolved to be humble, and the first thing you knew found yourself strutting with pride. You pledged yourself in your own heart, that no unclean thought or desire should cross the threshold of your soul's habitation, and the first thing you knew your imagination had taken wing and gone away into unclean and forbidden realms. Yes, and in your struggle for the mastery over this condition of things, you have been made to say in the anguish of your hearts, 'O wretched man that I am! who shall deliver me from the body of this death.' How are we to account for this state of things among Christians? The Apostle Paul tells us plainly that it is, '*Sin that dwelleth in me.*' 'Well, but,' says one, 'Paul is here describing the sinner.' This cannot be, for he says: '*I delight in the law of God after the inward man,*' and this the sinner does not do. The sinner is dead in trespasses and in sin, he is dominated both by Satan and the carnal mind. He 'rolls sin' of his own free choice, 'as a **sweet** morsel under his tongue.' He has no inward man in his state of spiritual death, 'delighting in the law of God.'

"Please, your Honor, the Scriptures and fundamental facts in human nature do not contradict each other. And the condition of things described here by the apostle is in perfect harmony with the facts in Christian experience. Hence the necessity for the second work of grace, the baptism of the Holy Ghost after pardon, in order to entire sanctification, or cleansing from the *carnal mind*, the *body of death*, the '*sin that dwelleth in me.*' And thanks be to God through Jesus Christ, our Lord, whose blood cleanseth from all sin, this pollution of our natures can all be taken away. I appeal to the Christian people in this hall to-night, have you not been singing:

'Prone to wander, Lord, I feel it:
Prone to leave the God I love?'

"You love God, but you feel prone to leave Him. Is this not a singular condition of things? And you, without exception, bear me witness that it is true. This proneness to wander from the God you love, is accounted for because 'ye are yet carnal,' and the carnal mind is 'enmity against God; it is not subject to the law of God, neither indeed can be.' Then according to Romans 6: 6: 'Let your old man be crucified with Him (Christ), chat the *body of sin* might

be destroyed.' Then you will no more be singing:
'Prone to wander, Lord, I feel it.' It is the carnal
mind remaining in the Christian; the carnal mind,
which is not, cannot be subject to the will of God,
that makes you cry out: 'When I would do good,
evil is present with me,' 'O, wretched man that I
am,' and 'prone to wander, Lord, I feel it.' All of
this indwelling sin, this disturbing element in the
believer's breast is taken out by the baptism of the
Holy Ghost, in entire sanctification; and this baptism
of the Holy Ghost never falls on sinners, but only on
believers, purifying their hearts by faith. This I
will show you from the Scriptures. Take the words
of Jesus in John 8th chapter, 37th to 39th verse. 'If
any man thirst, let him come unto me, and drink. He
that believeth on me, as the Scripture hath said,
Out of his belly shall flow rivers of living water.
(But this spake He of the Spirit, which they that
believe on Him should receive: for the Holy Ghost
was not yet given).' How plain are these Scriptures!
In what beautiful harmony with the promise of John
the Baptist: 'He shall baptize you with the Holy
Ghost and with fire.'

"We see here a second grace promised to those
who believed on Him, but had not yet received the
gift of the Holy Ghost. Notice this gift was not for
sinners, but for believers. Now take another Scripture, John 14: 15, 'If you love me, keep my command-

ments, and I will pray the Father, and He shall give you another Comforter, that He may abide with you forever. Even the Spirit of truth, whom the world cannot receive, because it seeth Him not, neither knoweth Him; but ye know Him, for He dwelleth with you, and shall be in you.' I call attention to the fact that the Holy Ghost is here promised to *believers*, the disciples of our Lord. Christ never would have said to sinners; 'If ye love me, keep my commandments.'

" Not only is the Spirit promised to believers, but Jesus declares plainly that none but believers can receive Him, 'whom the world cannot receive,' that is, the unpardoned, the unregenerate. Jesus, only, can baptize with the Holy Ghost, and He makes no mistakes. He only bestows the Spirit upon His disciples, those that believe in, love and obey Him.

"In the 17th chapter of John we hear our Lord praying for the *sanctification* of His disciples, and for them, also, which shall believe on Him through their word. This prayer of our Lord was answered on the day of Pentecost, when the Holy Ghost came suddenly upon the disciples, purifying their hearts by faith, and empowering them for service.

"We now call attention to Acts, 8th chapter. Here we learn that Philip preached the word in the city of Samaria, 'and the people with one accord gave heed unto those things which Philip spake,' and there was great joy in that city.' Why was there 'great joy'? Simply because the people received the pardon of their sins. You may rest assured that the preaching of Philip did not make *sinners* rejoice. It is a plain case. They believed and were saved, for the inspired writer says: ' But when they believed Philip preaching the things concerning the kingdom of God, and the name of Jesus Christ, they were baptized, both men and women.' This explains why there was joy among them.

" ' Now, when the apostles, which were at Jerusalem, heard that Samaria had received the Word of God, they sent unto them Peter and John, who, when they were come down, prayed for them that they might receive the Holy Ghost, for as yet He was fallen upon none of them.' Fortunate Samaritans! We can name plenty of modern ecclesiastics, who would have said to them: 'You got it all when you were converted, and there is no such thing as a second instantaneous work of grace.' Peter and John knew far better than this, and if you will look down in the 17th verse you will see that the Samaritans received the Holy Ghost. But, says some one, we see that the Scriptures clearly teach that the baptism of the Holy Ghost is subsequent to pardon, and for believers only; but where is your Scripture for the assertion that the baptism of the Holy Ghost purifies the heart? Turn to Acts 15:8-9. Peter is explaining that God called him to preach to the Gentiles, and that he had fixed His seal upon his ministry to them. 'And God, which knoweth the hearts, bear them witness, giving them the Holy Ghost, even as He did unto us; and put no difference between us and them, purifying their hearts by faith.' This Scripture makes it quite plain that both on the day of Pentecost and at the house of Cornelius there was a purifying of hearts by the baptism of the Holy Ghost. The opposers of the second work of grace, when hard pressed, have tried to make it appear that Cornelius was a sinner up to the time the Holy Ghost fell upon him. That can not be, for Jesus said the 'world,' the unpardoned, could not receive the Holy Ghost. 'This spake He of the Spirit, which THEY that *believed* on Him should receive.' Sinners never receive the baptism of the Holy Ghost. Besides, the Scriptures abundantly show that Cornelius was a 'DEVOUT man.' There are no devout sinners. He 'feared God with all his house,' and 'prayed always.' He 'worked righteousness,' and was accepted of God. To call such a man a sinner is to do violence to the plain teaching of God's word. But he had not yet been sanctified wholly; he yet needed the *purity* of his *heart* by the baptism of the Holy Ghost, and this he received instantaneously under the preaching of Peter, not at regeneration, for he was already regenerated, not by growth, not by death, but by *faith*. (Applause.) My friends, I could stand here all night and read you Scriptures, and cite you incidents and experiences recorded in the Bible, that prove beyond doubt that sanctification from all sin, or the baptism of the Holy Ghost, purifying the heart by faith, is an instantaneous work wrought in the believer's heart, subsequent to regeneration.

"But for the present I shall rest the case, and now I want every person, Christian and sinner, in this hall who believes that I have shown from the Scriptures that full salvation, or the baptism of the Holy Ghost, is a second work of grace, to rise to your feet." Instantly the entire audience arose. "And now," said Huton, "I want every Christian in this audience who desires to be sanctified wholly to meet me about this platform for a closing prayer." Hicks was sitting on the first seat in front of Huton. He made one step forward, the power fell on him, and he rushed into Huton's arms, and while the two lawyers stood embracing each other, the people wept, and some of the old Christians shouted for joy. Not less than fifty people came forward for prayer, several were saved, and although the meeting lasted until late the eager congregation remained to see the conclusion of the services. Finally Huton announced that the protracted services would begin at the store the next evening and dismissed the congregation, just at the time the cake-walk broke up at the church. As old Sister True passed by the church on her way home from the City Hall, Sister Dishrattler was coming out of the church, and Sister True said, "Oh, Sister Dishrattler, you ought to have been at the meeting at the City Hall to-night." As Sister Dishrattler hurried away home to get the back hall ready for the young people to have their dance, she said, "Indeed I do not think so, I propose to be truly loyal to my church myself. Others can run after every fanaticism that comes along if they want to, but as for me and mine we are *Methodists*, and nothing will ever draw us away from our church."

CHAPTER XI.

VICTORY.

Saturday evening the first service of the holiness meeting at the store was held at half past seven o'clock.

Dr. Gall was in the city and he and Mr. Youngduck did all in their power to keep the people from attending the meetings. Many worldly-minded Methodists joined in with them, and not a few good people who were really anxious to attend the meeting for the spiritual benefit they hoped to derive, were whipped into line, on the plea of loyalty to the church, and were induced to promise that they would not attend the meeting. Notwithstanding the opposition, the store was packed to its utmost capacity. Huton read Wesley's sermon on "Sin in Believers," gave an earnest exhortation for seekers, and the improvised altar was filled at once. Quite a number of back-sliders were reclaimed, two souls were powerfully sanctified and several sinners were converted.

It was announced that there would be a sunrise prayer-meeting at the store; also meetings at three in the afternoon, and half past seven in the evening. Dr. Gall sent a loyal local preacher to hold his quarterly meeting, and remained in Newton to help Mr.

Youngduck in the work of hindering the revival at the store as much as possible.

Sabbath morning the DEAR YOUNG PEOPLE who had been much worn out with CHURCH WORK the night of the cake walk, and the dance which followed, were able to get out and climb up in the choir loft. They took up most of the hour with songs, and Dr. Gall did not read his text until twenty minutes to twelve. His subject was "Evolution." The sermon was respectable only because of its old age. The doctor had absorbed the sermon from Wilford Hall's "Problem of Human Life, Here and Hereafter," published some twenty years ago, and it had done faithful service around three different districts. He labored for the first half hour to prove that men are not monkeys, and but for the giggling, grinning choir back of him, would have made a better impression, but with such specimens before them, not a few in the audience seemed to have grave doubts on the subject. The last half of the sermon was devoted to a tirade against the holiness movement.

Sabbath afternoon and evening many people were turned away from the store for want of standing room. In the afternoon Huton read Mr. Wesley's sermon, "The Circumcision of the Heart," and for the evening service he read Mr. Wesley's sermon on "Christian Perfection."

The afternoon service was good, but the evening

meeting was a time of great power. Most of the people blessed at the altar were respectable church members, who found under Wesley's searching sermons that their religion was a mere form. Some of them had been converted years before, but had lost their first love, then fallen into a lukewarm state, and from that had become entirely backslidden in heart. While their lives had been respectably moral, spiritually they were dead. Worst of all they were not aware of their perilous condition.

Dr. Poolkins' sermons on the "Modern Holiness Craze." and Dr. Gall's sermons on "Monerons" and "Monkeys" had utterly failed to awaken them from their carnal sleep. Others who had been in the church for years, and trying after a fashion to do their duty, but knew nothing of the new birth, were mightily convicted for sin, and called on God for mercy, and mercy came.

But few received the blessing of sanctification at first, for there were but few in a justified state. Monday afternoon many members of the various churches were at the store, and Huton read Mr. Wesley's sermon, " A Call to Back-sliders."

The first paragraph of the sermon, read in Huton's strong, clear voice made many hearts to quake. He repeated it in slow, solemn tones: " Presumption is one grand snare of the devil, in which many of the children of men are taken. They so presume upon

the mercy of God, as utterly to forget his justice.
Although he has expressly declared: 'Without holiness no man shall see the Lord,' yet they flatter
themselves, that in the end, God will be better than
his word. They imagine that they may live and die
in their sins, and nevertheless escape the damnation
of hell." There was more real, unadulterated, awful
truth in that paragraph, than many of the poor
deluded people had heard in years. No wonder heads
went down all over the audience. Before the sermon was finished many people were weeping. The
altar was filled at once, and not less than half a
score of precious souls who once had known the love
of Christ, but who had wandered far from Him were
powerfully reclaimed.

Monday evening Huton read Mr. Wesley's sermon
on "The Wedding Garment." The sermon is not a
long one. Huton read it with peculiar power; the
Spirit of the Lord was in the place. Although the
store was packed, and every particle of standing
room was occupied, an awful stillness was on the
people. When Huton came to the last paragraph in
the sermon which he had memorized, he laid down
the book and with shining face, and uplifted hands,
repeated it. "Holiness becometh his house forever.
This is the wedding garment of all who are called to
'the marriage of the Lamb.' Clothed in this they
will not be found naked. 'They have washed their

robes and made them white in the blood of the
Lamb.' But as to all of those who appear in the
last day without the wedding garment, the Judge
will say, 'Cast them into outer darkness; there shall
be weeping and gnashing of teeth.'" The scene
which immediately followed, I cannot describe.
People fell upon their knees in every part of the
building, and many cried aloud for mercy.

Huton called on his friend Hicks to lead in prayer,
and the man fell on his knees and mightily prevailed
with God. Sobs and shouts soon mingled in the tor-
rent of revival power that swept through the place.
The meeting lasted until near midnight, and when
it closed some thirty souls had been blessed: most of
them either reclaimed or converted.

Reader, I regret to have to record the fact, but
fact it is, and I must be true to history. While this
glorious work was going forward at the store, Dr.
Gall and Mr. Youngduck were over at the church in
the pastor's study planning how to head off the camp-
meeting in Huton's woods, smoking cigars, and telling vulgar stories.

The whole of Newton was stirred with the wonderful meetings at the store. Huton and Hicks gave
up their office work entirely for the present, and
went from place to place in the city to pray with
and talk to the people.

Many of the Methodist *reconcentrados* broke out of

the *trocha* Dr. Gall and Mr. Youngduck had built around them and went to the store, seeking food for their starving souls

I must mention a young shoe merchant, a steward in Central Church, who, becoming deeply interested in the subject of salvation, called at Huton's residence by engagement for a personal talk with the lawyer.

Mr. Jones said, "I admit that the Lord is with you people. I have religion and sense enough to know that these meetings you are holding at the store are of God. You could not do the work you are doing there without divine help, and I am not satisfied with my own experience. But I have always been prejudiced against sanctification. I have never been able to see how it is that people can get to be so good that they can not be tempted, or sin or grow any more in grace, and that, as I understand, is what the holiness people teach."

HUTON: "Did you ever hear a holiness preacher preach that, or anyone in the experience say they were in a state where they could not be tempted, or could not sin, or grow in grace?"

MR. JONES: "Well, no, I never did. The truth is I never mixed up with the holiness people, but that is what they teach, so I am informed; that is correct, is it not?"

HUTON: "Yes, I have often heard all these

things charged against the holiness people, but there is not a word of truth in it. Sanctification does not destroy the devil, my brother, it destroys the carnal mind. The devil remains the same and continues to tempt sanctified people. But it is no sin to be tempted. The sin consists in yielding to temptation. Our Saviour was tempted, but he did not sin. This charge brought against the holiness people that they claim they can not be tempted is the merest nonsense. Brother Jones, hereafter when you hear that charge brought against us, please to contradict it on the spot. The people who oppose us ought to be honest at least. They certainly know by this time that no sanctified person claims that he or she is beyond temptation. Of course some one might say, I can not be tempted to drink whiskey. Well, such a one would not mean that whiskey could not be offered them, but they simply mean that they could not be induced to drink it, see? Well, so with reference to all temptation."

MR. JONES: "I see the point, and I am glad you explained it to me, but is it not true that the sanctified people claim that they do not want to sin?"

HUTON: "No doubt of their saying that. But what Christian does? You claim to be justified, Brother Jones. Do you want to sin?"

MR. JONES: "No indeed, I do not. I want to

keep from sin, but I find a strong inclination within me to do so some times."

HUTON: "Exactly. Now, when one is sanctified wholly that strong inclination is taken out of him, and you will never more hear him singing,

> 'Prone to wander, Lord, I feel it,
> Prone to leave the God I love.'"

MR. JONES: "I see the point, but the main question is this, can a man ever sin again after he has once had the carnal mind taken out of him?"

HUTON: "Most assuredly he can. Sanctification does not destroy a man's free agency. If God placed a man in a condition where he could not sin, there would be no virtue in resisting temptation. Man would be a mere stock, you see, and not capable of making a choice, good or bad. A pure being is a free being, and can resist temptation, and remain pure, or yield to temptation, and fall from the state of purity. Adam was pure, and he sinned. Some of the angels, who were pure, kept not their first estate, but sinned and fell."

MR. JONES: "I see. That all seems plain enough, but one more question. Do not the holiness people teach that there is no such thing as Christian growth after sanctification?"

HUTON: "They do not. On the contrary, they teach that growth in grace is far more easy and rapid after sanctification than before. The carnal mind, which is enmity against God, has been destroyed, which of course is the principal hindrance to growth, so you see that sanctification, instead of putting an end to growth, is really the beginning of substantial and eternal growth."

MR. JONES: "Well, how is it that the holiness people are so fearfully misrepresented?"

HUTON: "Ignorance and prejudice, my brother, are at the bottom of all of it."

MR. JONES: "I have no doubt that is true. I am glad to have had this talk with you. What is the best paper I could get to post me thoroughly on the subject?"

HUTON: "THE PENTECOSTAL HERALD, published in Louisville, Ky., a sixteen page weekly, price $1.00 per year, is the paper for you. I will cheerfully send in your name and money."

MR. JONES: "All right, here is the dollar, send it in at once. But, honest, do you not think this holiness movement will split the Southern Methodist Church?"

HUTON: "Not a bit of it. Those of us who believe the doctrine do not intend to go out, and we do not intend to be put out, or do anything to be put out for. The anti-holiness element will not go out, and we do not intend to put them out, so you see there is no chance for a separation."

MR. JONES: "But I understand they will put you

people out. The preachers say your character will be arrested for contumacious conduct as soon as this meeting is over, what will you do about that?"

HUTON: "Well, if they put me out in a legal way, I will join the church again at once. There are a score of preachers in the Conference who would gladly take me in. If they put me out in an illegal way, I will appeal the case, and arrest the whole outfit for mal-administration, and they will be glad enough to compromise, and put me back in the church, if I will agree not to prosecute. Oh they are practically helpless. All they do on the line of persecution only awakens sympathy, and stirs up greater interest in the movement."

MR. JONES: "I see you are on top of the log which ever way it happens to turn. But I understand the bishops are all against you people."

HUTON: "I don't know, perhaps that is true, but that does not matter much. You know a Methodist Bishop has not the influence over the people he used to have. This is a country of the people. We do not worship ecclesiastics here like they do in Europe. There is a class of course who let the ecclesiastics do their religious thinking for them, but that class do not amount to much in a religious way. They have a good deal of churchianity but are not much on Christianity. The bishops come around once in awhile, and we are glad to see them, but they do not own the church by any manner of means, and if they continue to oppose the doctrine of entire sanctification for the next ten years as they have the past ten, their prestige will be almost entirely gone, and it will be little more credit to a man to be a bishop, than it now is to be presiding elder. Oh yes, it is entirely possible that ten years from now if a man of the first rank in the Southern Methodist ministry should be elected bishop, he would not permit himself to be ordained. The office has not half the prestige and influence to-day that it had twenty years ago.

"The one thing, of course, that keeps it up at all is the appointing power. Of course any man who has from five hundred to a thousand positions to fill with an influential class of men, with salaries ranging all the way from three hundred, to three thousand dollars a year, will always have a certain kind of influence over a certain class of men. The truth is, Brother Jones, when you take holiness out of Methodism, our system of church government is a very dangerous one.

"Give us bishops and presiding elders, sanctified from all sin, full of faith and the Holy Ghost, and we are safe, but let us discard these Bible truths once so dear to the Methodists, and ambition and selfishness are bound to manifest themselves. A sort of ecclesiastical politics would be developed among us, with all sorts of wire pulling for the best appointments, and the result would be most degrading to ministerial character.

"No man is really fit for bishop or presiding elder who is not a wholly sanctified man. Methodist machinery cannot possibly run smoothly unless it is well lubricated with the oil of full salvation.

"The holiness people are prepared, however, for whatever may come. This is a free country, you know, and the Methodist Church is the church of the people, the church of the masses, the last people in the world to submit to ecclesiastical tyranny."

MR. JONES: "Well, I am with you in sentiment. I hope to be in the experience also soon. Pray for me, and be sure to send for my paper."

Mr. Jones left Huton's with an entirely different view of the situation from anything he had had before.

I should like to dwell at length on the store meetings, but time and space will not permit. I must not close, however, without telling the reader of the remarkable conversion of a noted gutter drunkard. He was known about the streets as "Keg-sucker John." No one seemed to know or care anything of John's antecedents. He and his companion, "Whiskey Jim," had been familiar figures about the streets of Newton for many years.

The bar-rooms and low dives were their familiar

haunts. Their principal industry was to gather mint from a branch on the outskirts of the city, and trade it at the bar-room counters for whiskey. John had applied to him the name of Keg-sucker, because it was his habit to prowl about in the early morning from one bar-room to another, and suck from the bung holes of beer kegs the few drops of beer that had been left in the kegs that were emptied during the night and pitched out at the side door.

Keg-sucker John and Whiskey Jim were devoted friends. Someone said if you wanted to find both of the poor bloats, you need seek but one of them, the other could always be found near by.

When the meetings commenced in the store, John became intensely interested in them, and shambled about the store door, listening as best he could from the outside. Hicks noticed him there and induced him to go inside. To the surprise of all, John was soon at the altar of prayer. He seemed to fully realize his condition, and making a full surrender, was soon most powerfully converted; another trophy for Christ, won by the holiness movement from among the most hopeless class of the lost.

Whiskey Jim was deeply affected by John's conversion, and although John and many of the holiness people put forth most earnest efforts to rescue him, poor Jim seemed to be hopelessly joined to his idols.

John, a few days after his conversion, went to

the altar seeking sanctification, and received the
blessing, attended by great demonstration of the
Spirit. John was so changed both inside and out,
that he attracted much attention about the city.
Huton gave him a good suit of clothes, and he became
one of the most conspicious figures at the store
meetings. To the surprise of everyone he could
sing well, and was either shouting or singing from
morning till night. By common consent the word
"Keg-sucker" was dropped, and the word "Happy,"
took its place, and now John was known by all as
"Happy John."

He secured a position as porter in a grocery store
and when not at religious meetings, was at his post
of duty in the grocery.

At two strides Happy John stepped from the low-
est place in the gutter to that of a special favorite
with the entire population of Newton. Saint and
sinner, police, and the various members of the city
court, in fact everyone, except a few barkeepers,
seemed to be interested in Happy John. It was
pathetic to see him labor for Whiskey Jim's salvation, and although he could not get Jim to forsake
his sins, he put comfortable clothes on him, and got
him a comfortable place to sleep, and although Jim
frequently sold the clothes given him by Happy John
for whiskey, his old companion in sin seemed never
to tire of the effort to rescue the poor drunkard.

Most any night after the meetings closed at the store, Happy John could be seen down among the dives seeking for Jim, and leading him off to the little room he had fitted up for him, where he would give him some food, saved from his own supper, and then get him to bed, and frequently fall asleep on the floor at Jim's bedside, after exhausting himself, physically, in prayer.

There were many other notable salvations, but I must hasten to close this chapter.

The meetings continued in the store for three weeks, and then had to close that the merchant who had rented the room might move in his stock of goods. Huton sometimes read one of Wesley's sermons, frequently gave the people a Bible reading, and at some of the services simply had prayer, songs and testimonies, followed with altar work.

Happy John was one of the best workers the last half of the meeting. More than two hundred souls were either converted, reclaimed or sanctified. The city was mightily stirred, and many of the NEW Methodists were surprised to find that, after all, John Wesley was not the ordinary, changeable, vacillating sort of a man they had supposed him to be.

Dr. Gall and Mr. Youngduck fought the meetings from start to finish, and one week after the meeting closed at the store, they started a protracted meeting at the Central Church. Dr. Gall announced at the first service that there would be no excitement or fanaticism permitted in the meetings, but everything should be done in decency and order.

The cake walkers sat up behind the pulpit and sang. Dr. Gall and Mr. Youngduck took turn about preaching. The staple of their preaching was abuse and ridicule of "Modern Sanctification." On the Sabbath night when the meetings closed, Dr. Gall said he had heard much of a store revival; he understood that many sinners had been saved there; doubtless if such was the case, they would want to join some church. Now would be a good time to measure the length of that store meeting. The doors of the church were opened. Of course no one went forward.

A week later the Conference organ contained an item from Newton headed, "Times of Refreshing," which read as follows: "We have just closed a week's meeting at Central Church, in Newton. Our beloved Presiding Elder, Rev. Josephus Gall, D. D., did most of the preaching, which is equivalent to saying, it was well done. While there was no undue excitement, and no effort to produce any, the intelligent, LOYAL people were much instructed and edified by the able sermons of our Presiding Elder.

"Dr. Gall is a tower of strength on his district. He looks carefully after every interest of the church, and handles shams without gloves. It might be well to say just here that there has been much talk about a so-called holiness meeting in this city. I need not go into details, but will simply say, that one week after this store meeting closed, special invitation was made for any and all persons converted in those meetings to join our church, and not one joined. The thoughtful will make a note of this. These meetings held on eccentric lines do no good, but only hurt the church. Yours in loyalty and love,

"FREDERIC CLARK HARRIS YOUNGDUCK."

Weekly holiness meetings were held from house to house among the people, in which many souls were converted and sanctified, and the effect of the store meetings spread all through the city, awakening and developing spiritual life in every quarter.

CHAPTER XII.

OPPOSITION — ALLIES.

There is this remarkable feature about the opposition to the great holiness revival. It matters not how many souls may be saved in one of these holiness meetings, or how great the demonstrations of the Holy Ghost, the opposition to the doctrine of instantaneous sanctification, subsequent to regeneration, seem to be absolutely blind to it all, and their battle cry constantly is, "On with the opposition!"

The miracles of the Holy Ghost, wrought in the souls of men, cleansing them from all sin, seem to have no more effect on those who do not believe in instantaneous sanctification, than the miracles of Christ wrought on the bodies of men, had on the rulers of the Jewish Church two thousand years ago.

Take the case of Rev. G. Q. Totum, D. D. It is said by those who know him best that he has never been known to win a soul from sin to Christ, in fact, he said not long since to a friend of this writer, that if there had been a sinner converted under his ministry in the past thirty years he knew nothing of it. Yet Dr. Totum has the best appointments in his conference, smokes cigars, tells anecdotes, fights holiness, and goes on his way seemingly with no

regret that his own ministry is so barren of any visible results.

Worse still, he has been one of the most aggressive men in the church to hunt down. persecute,
revoke licenses of local preachers, or expel men from
the ministry and the church for holding meetings in
halls or groves for the conversion of sinners, and the
sanctification of believers.

Dr. Totum is so bitterly prejudiced against the
holiness movement, and especially against holiness
camp-meetings, that he could not rejoice if a thousand of his fellowmen were happily converted from
sin at a holiness camp-meeting. Think of it! A
minister of the gospel, and yet so bitter against
these holiness meetings that if he should hear of a
multitude of sinners being saved in one of them,
instead of rejoicing with them, he becomes indignant, and sets about devising some plan to expel
from the church those under whose ministry and
labors they were saved.

The reader may think on these things and draw
his own conclusions.

The great revival at the store, as the reader has
seen from Dr. Gall's remarks at church, and Mr.
Youngduck's letter to the church paper, was no
exception to the rule.

Through the constant efforts of Dr. Gall and the
young pastor, not a few members of Central Church

were aroused to a state of very bitter prejudice against "second blessingists," for this was the name applied to all those baptized by the Holy Ghost.

The large element of dancers, theater goers, and card players in Central Church were almost a unit in their unbelief in the second work of grace. In Central Church there were several influential men who owned part interest in race horses, and always attended the fall races, and quite a number who dealt in futures and various gambling methods. All of these rallied around Dr. Gall in his efforts to head off the proposed camp-meeting in Huton's woods. Letters were written to the church papers, and for the secular press, pointing out the disloyalty and harm of such meetings. The hope was confidently expressed that the next Annual Conference would pass a set of iron-clad resolutions against all such innovations, and the opposers settled it to their hearts' content that if the church could hold itself together, and the country could patiently endure the plague of holiness meetings in stores, halls, and woods until the next General Conference met, the whole matter would be disposed of in short order, and then, with the exception of the little disturbance with Spain, peace and quiet would be restored to the country once more, and no sort of holiness meetings would ever again dare to molest or make back-slidden Methodists afraid.

Meanwhile the preparations for the camp-meeting went forward with great vigor. Happy John could hardly wait for the time of the meetings to roll around. At the head of a large number of working men he went out one Saturday afternoon and cleared up about twenty-five acres of land for the encampment, simply raking away all leaves and trash, taking out the small grubs, and cutting the low limbs from the trees, leaving good shade for the campers.

Evangelist Sampson, with his excellent singer, and three experienced lay workers, had been engaged to conduct the meetings. The time was set for August 15th to 25th, and the meetings were thoroughly advertised. A large three-pole tent, that could seat 4,000 people, was secured and erected in an excellent position in the center of the grounds cleared for the purpose. Three long rows of tents for campers, enclosed three sides of the audience tent, standing back from it a distance of fifty yards. Electric light wires were run out to the grounds, and pipes from the city water works were laid, so that of good water there was an abundant supply for man and beast. A large bell was fastened to the limb of a giant oak, with which to rouse the worshipers. Many campers moved out to the grounds Wednesday afternoon, and Thursday the camp was a busy scene of life. The long rows of white tents made a beautiful appearance under the thick shade of the great spreading trees, quite novel to those who had never had the privilege of visiting a camp-meeting.

Wagons were coming and going; campers were fixing up their furniture, and arranging everything so that they might be ready for the first regular service, Friday evening, at 7:30.

Happy John got leave of absence from the store, and put in his entire time out at the camp ground, helping anyone who had need of assistance. Thursday evening there was such a large number of persons on the grounds, that Happy John was asked to conduct a prayer service under the big tent, which he did, and the people had a glad, happy time. Thursday afternoon the *Newton Times Star* contained the following communication:

"TO ALL LOVERS OF LAW AND ORDER.

"We, the undersigned, wish the public to distinctly understand that the Southern Methodist Church is in no way connected with, or responsible for the so-called holiness camp-meeting to be held near this city.

"On the contrary, we have done all in our power to prevent the holding of these meetings, and we now say that all persons claiming membership in the Southern Methodist Church, who conduct, or take part in said meetings, lay themselves liable to trial and expulsion from the church on the charge of contumacious and disrespectful conduct toward their superiors in office. We also ask all lovers of law and order of all creeds, to keep away from these meetings.

"REV. JOSEPHUS GALL. D.D., P. E.

"REV. FREDERIC CLARK HARRIS YOUNGDUCK, P.C."

This letter was a fine advertisement for the camp-meeting. No one, not even the holiness opposers, supposed for a moment that Dr. Gall or Mr. Young-duck could in any way contribute to the success of a revival of true religion, and no one who expected to attend the meetings regretted that these two clergymen would not be present.

Christians and sinners alike condemned the action of the opposing preachers. "If they can do nothing themselves to save men, and it seems they can not," said a leading merchant, "they ought at least let those alone who can and will help men to a Christian life. I am not a Christian myself, but this holiness meeting down here at the store, stirred up this town as it has not been stirred before since I came to live in it, twenty years ago. These lawyers, Hicks and Huton, are men of sense, and evidently have but one object in view, the making of men better. It is useless for anyone to try to make the impression on the minds of the people of Newton, that these men have any purpose to violate the law of the church, or show contempt for legitimate authority; at the same time, they will not surrender their religious or civil rights, because of the bluster of petty, ecclesiastical tyrants.

"I for one, had not thought much of the meetings, until all this noise of opposition was raised, but now my sympathies are enlisted. I gave Hicks $20.00 this morning to help defray the expenses of the meeting, and I have rented one of the tents and intend to take my family out and enjoy the meetings."

This merchant voiced the sentiments of many of the best people of the city. In fact, the published letter in the *Times Star* was an excellent advertisement for the meetings.

In his opposition to the holiness camp-meetings, Dr. Gall had in Newton one powerful ally, of whom at this time he knew nothing.

Next to Dr. Gall and Mr. Youngduck, this man of whom we speak, was the most bitter against the camp-meeting, of all persons in Newton. His name was Jack Hess. Hess had the largest and most palatial barroom in Newton. His custom was large; he kept several bartenders behind his counters, and from a financial point of view, did a successful business. Hess was fully six feet high, and broad in proportion, with low forehead, small wicked eyes, and heavy jaws. He wore fine clothes, drove fast horses, paid his bills promptly, spent his money freely, and while it can be truthfully said that no one loved him, and many feared him, yet he had a large following.

and delighted to boss the gang that bowed without a murmur to his wishes. He was quite a power in city politics, and in this way came in contact with prominent men, which contributed no little to his pride and almost unbearable arrogancy.

Hess' barroom was the headquarters for quite a large element of the more respectable class of the toughs of the city of Newton.

On the Thursday evening of which we write, Hess sat with a company of chums at one of the tables in his barroom. "Say, boys," said Hess "There is some good reading in the *Times Star* this afternoon; let me read it to you." Everybody was silent in the barroom while Hess read Dr. Gall's manifesto against the camp-meeting. When he concluded, he said: "Now that is what I call hittin' em straight out from the shoulder. I hope the people of this city will take the parson's advice, and keep away from the place."

"No doubt you do," said a voice from over in one corner. Hess turned, and, looking in the direction from which it came, saw Whiskey Jim, sitting over a mug of beer.

"What are you doing in here, Jim?" said Hess in an angry tone. Without looking up from his crackers and beer, Jim said, "I crossed a dime in my travels to-day, and I knew you wanted it, so I just brought it around to you."

"Well, now keep quiet over there, and make yourself scarce," said Hess in an angry mood.

"I am willing to get out now if you'll jest tell me what is so wonderful good in that composition you bin readin," said Jim. Hess rose to his feet and said in a loud tone, "I don't know how the rest of you like it, but for my part, I think this man Gall is on the right track. What are all these churches standing around here for? They cost a big lot of money and they are empty most of the time. If decent people want to worship, why do they not go to the churches for it? This store meeting down here was a disgrace to this city. I believe that such things ought to be done in decency and order myself."

"Yes, that store meetin' was everlastin' ruination to your business, Mr. Bigneck," said Jim. "You lost a dozen of your best customers, and I wish you had lost me, and you would if you haden't er had me on hands so long."

There was a big laugh in the barroom at Jim's remark. Hess had once, in one of the newspapers of the city, been called "Bigneck," and any such reference made him angry. The laugh which followed added fuel to the flame, and seizing a chair he started toward Jim, crying out in a rage, "Get out of here, you old street garbage, or I will drive your old bloated head down between your shoulders."

Just at that moment Happy John started in the barroom, and seeing the danger Jim was in, he leaped between him and Hess, catching hold of the chair, and said, "Hold, Mr. Hess, I will take care of Jim." "Well, take him out of here, and both of you keep clear of this place," said Hess. "Amen," said Happy John, as he helped Whiskey Jim from the door.

Beckoning a friend to follow, Hess retired into a room back of the barroom, ordering mixed drinks sent to them.

"It is hard for a gentleman to take jaw from such an old bloat as Whiskey Jim is," said Hess, "and as for that cur, Happy John, I've made up my mind to kill him, if he does not let me and my business alone. He has done more to hurt my trade since that crank meeting down at the store, than everything else in town. During the last week of that holiness meeting my trade fell off at least one half, and not less than eight or ten men, who used to spend from one to five dollars a week with us, have quit the place entirely. Those crazy loons sang and shouted, down at that store, until they had half the people of the city scared out of their wits. I would not have this holiness camp-meeting held in the Huton woods for one hundred dollars cool cash, and if they made a yearly thing of it, we had just as well hunt some other place for business. I hear old man Gall is going to get his big Convention, or Conference, or what you call it, to pass resolutions against the thing. I do hope he will. He and this Young-duck running around here after him will never do our trade any harm. Give us men like them, in the pulpits of the country, and our business is safe."

"Oh, I think you are worse scared than hurt," said Hess' friend. "I don't think the camp-meeting will hurt your business materially." "Which means that you don't know those holiness people. Why the last one of them is a prohibitionist, and you can't make them shut up. They will undertake anything on earth that they take a notion ought to be done. They would as soon tackle Newton for local option as not."

"Well, they could not carry it if they did," said the other.

"That is all good enough," said Hess, "but the agitation is unhealthy for trade, besides I would have to give away in drinks a barrel of whiskey, and a car load of beer. And this temperance fuss hurts a barkeeper's social and political influence more than you can imagine. Oh, if this holiness movement business is not stopped, it means great agitation and great loss for me."

"See here," said Hess, "mum is the word, but if Gall can't keep the silly people from going to that camp-meeting, the boys and myself will try our hand on them in a way that they will not forget us soon. We will make them a little visit Sunday night, and when we get through with them they won't be in a hurry to hold another holiness camp-meeting near Newton."

"What do you mean?" said Hess' confidant, "talk more plainly." Hess stooped forward and whispered in his chum's ear, "I have got the boys posted, and we have gathered a couple of barrels of stale eggs, rotten cabbage, and spoiled Irish potatoes, and we will cut their electric light wire, and give them eggs and potatoes for lunch, and something harder, don't you forget it," with which remark Hess took a scale's weight from the pocket of his sack coat, and pitched it into the air.

The man with whom Hess was talking, Karoon by name, noticed that the weight had on it the hundred pound mark, that a small piece had been broken out of one side, and that lead had been run into one of the holes in the weight to make it balance properly. He took the weight in his hand, looked at it, and handed it back to Hess. Hess chuckled, and said: "If that weight could get in a good lick on Happy John, as they call him, it would put an end to his shouting." Just at that time Hess was called to the front room, and the conversation was brought to an end.

The truth is simply this: Hess had arranged with

a party of twenty-five or thirty toughs to make an attack on the camp Sabbath night with eggs and potatoes, and try to break up the meetings. The sad results of the wicked undertaking will be disclosed in the following chapter.

CHAPTER XIII.

THE CAMP-MEETING.

It must be remembered that the two lawyers, Hicks and Huton, were men of spotless reputation, fine intelligence, and unswerving integrity. No two men had more influence in Newton and the surrounding country than these two.

The very fact that they were at the head of the holiness movement in Newton, claimed for it the attention of thoughtful Christian people of all denominations. Such laymen have taken an important part in the present great holiness revival, in all parts of the country, and have been invaluable to it.

Laymen of means and influence in the church, who have been wholly sanctified, in these troublesome times, have a rare opportunity to serve God and their fellow-men. They can establish camp-grounds, rent halls, purchase tents, distribute literature, and in many ways help forward the good work of full salvation. Their social and financial influence in the church virtually protects them against the hue and cry of the persecutors.

There are plenty of men who will delight to drive from the church a poor preacher, who would not for one moment think of undertaking to expel a rich and influential layman. While there had been worked up in Central Church considerable anti-holiness sentiment, Hicks and Huton had no need to fear that there would be any serious attempt to put them out of the church, but they gave this matter little thought, having committed it all to God.

The evangelist and his helpers arrived on the camp-ground Friday at noon, and were soon comfortably quartered in their tents, and resting preparatory to the opening of the campaign at 7:30 o'clock.

The interest in the meeting was intense. The opposition to it had aroused the entire population of the city. In stores, shops, banks, bakeries, barber shops, and barrooms the subject of conversation was the holiness camp-meeting.

The two lawyers were busily looking after all the details, and seeing that the campers were comfortable. In a large shed, conveniently located, there were several cooking stoves, brought out by some of the good women of Newton, so that the campers from a distance could cook their food conveniently. One farmer had hauled in several barrels of apples, and placed them under the shed, with a card tacked on one of the barrels, "Free for All." A great heap of potatoes, and several large baskets of beans had been contributed by others. There was good fellowship on all sides, and the people were happy.

The spirit of "Old time religion" was in the very

air, and desire and expectation kindled a great flame of faith upon the altars of many hearts. The opposition to the meeting had stirred up the hearts of the Christians and they had been much in prayer. The victory had been fairly won before the bell sounded out the call to the first service.

There were not fewer than five thousand people on the grounds at the first service. Happy John had been detailed to lead the sunset prayer-meeting under a large persimmon tree, on a little knoll about two hundred yards from the big tent, and to ring the bell for all the services.

Hess and his gang were out on Friday evening, skulking about the grounds and planning for their mischief for the following Sabbath evening.

The first service was a time of great power. Saints rejoiced, and sinners hastened to the altar. Many believers were there also, seeking entire cleansing, and not a few were blessed. All day Saturday the tide was rising, every country road contributed to the great river of humanity that poured along the main thoroughfare that led to Huton's Camp-ground.

The whole twenty-five acres that had been cleared off for campers, was filled up, and Saturday evening Happy John and a number of men took their axes and cut out the undergrowth, so that room was made for many wagons that came in from all the country round, to spend the Sabbath. The scene was beauti-

ful to behold. Camp fires were burning in every
direction; busy wives were preparing the evening
meal, the men were caring for their teams, the
merry laugh of children was ringing through the
woods; songs of victory mingled with shouts of praise
at the big tent, could be heard in all parts of the
encampment, and best of all, there was among all
the people a sense of the presence of the invisible
Holy One. This consciousness pervaded the whole
place and people. Sinners seemed to be convicted
as soon as they arrived on the grounds, and those
believers who had not been sanctified wholly, felt
the hungering and thirsting rising in their hearts, to
be filled with righteousness. The sun was gone
down, Happy John had marched through the encampment singing,

> "Glory, glory, Jesus saves me,
>   Glory, glory to the lamb,
> Oh, the cleansing blood has reached me,
>   Glory, glory to the lamb,"

And a great throng had followed him to the persimmon tree, where on their faces they were calling
on God for victory.

Jack Hess and his lieutenants were in a little
room back of Hess' saloon, planning the Sabbath
night attack on the camp, and Dr. Gall and Mr.
Youngduck were on the back porch at Sister Dish-

rattler's smoking cigars and drawing up a paper to present to the Annual Conference, forbidding "Southern Methodist people attending, or in any way assisting in the so-called holiness camp-meetings."

The Saturday evening service was a time of wonderful power. But I need not try to describe it. No pen can put a holiness camp-meeting on paper.

The great tent was packed with people, multitudes stood around listening with close attention, scores of men and boys sat upon the straw in the altar, and there was a fervent and eager interest, which gave the speaker remarkable ease and liberty. Besides these favorable human conditions, the Lord had anointed the evangelist to preach the gospel of full salvation, and the Word was proclaimed with marvelous power and effect. At times the shouts of the people would almost drown the voice of the speaker. At such times he would pause for a few moments, and then launch again into the subject. He proved in a few clear sentences that God required HOLINESS in his LAW, and provided for HOLINESS in his GOSPEL. That God could not, in the nature of things, require less in his LAW, or provide for less in his GOSPEL.

I remember one striking paragraph of the preacher's sermon, word for word, as it fell from his lips:

"The Scriptures positively declare, 'This is the will of God, even your sanctification,' and I positively declare that God can not be a holy being and will anything less than the holiness of his intelligent creatures.

"Can you conceive of a sober father willing that his son shall be a drunkard, or an honest father willing that his son shall be a thief, or a truthful father willing that his son shall be a liar? — impossible. Neither can you conceive of a holy God willing that any one of his intelligent, immortal creatures shall be corrupt and unholy in heart or life.

"A blow struck at holiness is a blow struck at the very foundation of the Divine government. Yes, it is a blow struck at God Himself. To say that God does not will us to be holy, or that Jesus Christ, with his sin-cleansing blood, can not, or will not, make us holy, and that the Holy Ghost can not or will not bear witness to the blessed work when it is accomplished, is to pronounce an infamous slander upon the whole Godhead. To say that we are entirely sanctified, when we are converted or pardoned, is to take square issue with the theological libraries of the world and with Christian experience, but worst of all, with the plainly written Word of God, which clearly teaches that the 'carnal mind,' the 'old man,' the 'body of death,' the 'root of bitterness,' remains in the regenerate, and must be cleansed away before we can enjoy that 'holiness without which no man shall see the Lord.'"

The preacher literally "shelled the woods." The sentences leaped from his lips like the well-directed fire of a ten-inch rifle in the American Navy, and fell with telling accuracy, unmasking the enemy's batteries of false theories, and sweeping away the refuge of lies behind which the "carnal mind" was finding refuge.

He took up a strategic position, and delivered a telling fire into the ranks of autocratic ecclesiastics who would not enter into Canaan themselves, and who were trying to hinder those who desired to enter in. He called upon the spiritual reconcentrados who had been corralled by Conference resolutions to prevent them from enjoying the delicious fruits of full salvation, to break away from the dictates of men, and hasten to partake of the "corn and wine, milk and honey, grapes and pomegranates," which had been so abundantly provided in the atonement made on Calvary. The silence in the vast throng was of that character of stillness which precedes a storm.

The preacher had his audience and took them with him to gaze for a moment on the first lovely pair in their original purity in the garden of Eden, before sin had stamped its foul stain upon their spotless spirits. Then they beheld with horror the first sin, and saw God's highly favored creatures fall into a state of moral defilement. They beheld with wonder, the arrangement for redemption wrought out in the mind of the infinite Father. They trembled while Sinai thundered forth the law, and waited with the patriarch the fulfillment of the promise that the seed of the woman should bruise the serpent's head.

They rejoiced with the shepherds on Judean hills, while the wise men followed the guiding star, and the angelic host shouted "Glory to God in the highest, peace on earth, good will to men." The preacher led the way, and the people followed on to the temptation in the Wilderness, and the glorious victory over Satan. They saw the lame leap at his word, the blind healed, and the dead raised up at his touch, and a legion of devils depart from their tortured victim at his command. They saw him feed the multitudes with the few loaves and small fishes, walk the waves of the tempest-tossed Galilee, and arise from his bed at night and go into the mountains to pray.

As the preacher advanced, and their souls caught fire, it seemed as if time and space were blotted out, and they saw Jesus bow himself in agony in the garden of Gethsemane, and stand, thorn-crowned, in purple robes before Pilate's judgment seat; they followed him to the cross, and standing afar off with the company of women, they saw him bleed and die.

They visited the sepulchre with Mary and found an empty tomb, and worshiped with the disciples at the feet of their risen Lord. They beheld him ascend into heaven, and heard the promise of the angels that in like manner he should return again. They heard of the white robes of the blood-washed company at the marriage supper of the Lamb.

And then it seemed that the clouds burst asunder, and all the bands of heaven played a triumphant march as Jesus descended upon the throne of universal empire, to reign over the people who had been sanctified with his precious blood. The people leaped and shouted for joy, sinners fell prone upon the ground, believers ran to the altar, some were sanctified before they fell upon their knees, others wrestled, Jacob-like, crying, "I will not let Thee go until Thou bless me." Those newly converted and sanctified, went through the audience shouting and exhorting sinners to come to Jesus, and believers to press over Jordan into the land of perfect love. Three hours swept by, and no one was tired; eleven o'clock came, and the preacher dismissed the people for the third time, and urged them to take some rest, and be refreshed for the coming conflict of the Sabbath day. Not less than fifty people lay down upon their cots that night, who since the going down of the sun, had either been pardoned or sanctified wholly.

With the twitter of the early bird on Sabbath

morning, Happy John arose and went out to the woods for prayer.

He felt a peculiar yearning in his heart for the salvation of poor old Whiskey Jim, and as he lay upon his face in the leaves, he said over and over, "I would gladly die if it would only bring Jim to Thee."

As he wrestled with Jesus, there stole into his heart a sense of victory, and he praised God for a full assurance that Jim would be saved during the meetings; he also had a strange impression that his own work was well nigh finished. He asked God for a text for the day, took his Testament from his pocket, opened it at random, and his eyes fell on these words of Jesus, in Luke 23:43: "TO-DAY SHALT THOU BE WITH ME IN PARADISE."

Happy John returned to the camp with a strange, quiet sweetness in his heart, which for immeasurable depth surpassed anything he had yet known. Just as the town clock in Newton struck six, Happy John rang the bell for morning prayer, and scores of worshipers arose, and dressed hurriedly and hastened to the great tent to win the assurance of victory for the day.

I shall not weary the reader's patience with an attempt at a description of the day's services. If you have attended a great holiness camp-meeting on the Sabbath day, when the glorious work was in full swing, you can easily picture the happy scenes of this Sabbath to yourself.

If you have never attended such a meeting, take a friend's advice and do not let another summer pass without visiting some one of the great holiness camp-meetings.

It must not be supposed that Dr. Gall and Mr. Youngduck were idle. Dr. Gall spent most of the day Saturday reading "The Problem" and other anti-holiness books and pamphlets, and preparing a sermon for Sabbath morning that he thought would certainly sweep the field and put an end to the holiness movement.

Mr. Youngduck spent the day on the streets, making the same little speeches in many stores, and to many people. On the streets everywhere, he was met with the question: "Why are you not out at the camp-meeting?" "What camp-meeting?" he would answer in a sort of innocent way. "Out at Huton's woods; the holiness camp-meeting. They are having a great time out there. I thought you Methodist preachers were great men for camp-meetings," would be the answer. Then with an air as if he did remember there was some such thing going on, Youngduck would say: "Oh, ah, yes, I believe they are having a meeting of some sort out in the woods; but it is not a Methodist meeting. Our church is in no way responsible for these meetings. You know

our church has given a deliverance on this subject.
Our bishops have spoken out against this whole
thing. They, with the leading men of our church,
are against the holiness movement and all this
fanaticism. I am a loyal Methodist, and when I can
not believe the doctrine and obey the discipline of
my church, I will leave it."

It would be impossible for me to tell how many
times Mr. Youngduck made this speech Saturday,
but the remark of a merchant, and a leading Baptist
of Newton, struck me forcibly. Youngduck had just
left this gentleman's store, where he had made his
speech, taking pains to state, "our bishops are all
against it."

"Well," said the Baptist brother, "I went to the
store meetings, and I was out at the camp-meeting
last night, and while I am free to confess that
I am not as religious as I ought to be, I have enough
religion to recognize it when I meet up with it, and
I tell you these people have the old time religion.
And this young fellow, Youngduck, in my judgment,
is very appropriately named. There is one thing
certain, he is not adding anything to the influence
of his bishops and his church in this city by the
manner in which he is acting.

"If I were a bishop, I would hate for it to be
generally known in any community, that I sided
with such men as Gall and Youngduck, on any

question, against such men as Hicks and Huton."

There was a point in the Baptist Brother's remark.
Many a little holiness fighter has gone about the
country for the last ten years, with tobacco juice on
his shirt front, and this well-worn sentence in his
mouth on all occasions, "Our bishops are all against
it." In this way the influence and prestige which
once belonged to Methodist Bishops has been irreparably damaged.

Dr. Gall labored hard and perspired freely Sabbath morning in his two hour's sermon in Central
Church. He was without unction. He tried hard to
speak with power, but only succeeded in storming.

Jack Hess, with a few of his pals, was sitting on
the back pew, listening to the discourse

I shall not try to give the doctor's sermon. It
was a tirade of abuse against evangelists, holiness
camp - meetings, and the PENTECOSTAL HERALD.
Among other things the doctor said: "Such meetings
as the one held in a store in this city, and the one
now being held in Huton's woods, ought to be declared
a nuisance, and be broken up by law; and I wonder
that the people do not stop them by force if necessary. I believe it will come to that yet. When men
will not listen to kindly entreaty, and walk rough
shod over ecclesiastical law, and decency, and order,
then it is time for the civil law to speak with the
voice of authority." Hess was highly pleased with

these remarks, and remained at the door to thank Dr. Gall for the sermon.

When the clan of toughs gathered at the barroom that evening to make preparation to move on the camp-ground, Hess told them of Dr. Gall's sermon, and assured them that they need fear no consequences that might follow, even if any one of them should be caught in the act of disturbing the worshipers in the woods.

As the company was leaving the barroom, Hess went behind the counter and took down from a shelf the scale weight, marked 100, with a piece broken out of one side, and lead run into the holes in the weight, in order to make it balance, and dropped it into his pocket.

Hess had instructed his men to surround the main tent, and just as the electric light went out, to fire a volley of decayed eggs and potatoes among the people; to direct their aim at the pulpit, to throw as fast as possible. yelling the meanwhile like Comanches; when they had expended their ammunition, to run for life, and meet in the little room back of the barroom, coming up an alley, and entering by a back door. He detailed two men who were not to throw eggs, but were to remain on the grounds for some time after the attack, and then bring word to the barroom with reference to the results.

The orders were well carried out. Hess and his

forces surrounded the main tent. It was a few minutes to eight o'clock when they stationed themselves
for action. Hess was standing near the pulpit, just
at the edge of the tent. A testimony meeting was
in progress. "It is almost time for preaching now,"
said the evargelist, "we wait a moment for anyone
else who may wish to speak." Happy John rose up;
he had been sitting in the straw in the altar, and he
now stood just to the right of the speaker's stand.
Hess was standing not more than ten feet from
John, and as John spoke, the barkeeper's eyes
glared upon him with the savageness of a wild beast.
Happy John said: "I do not know whether my friends
have noticed it, but I have been more quiet to-day
than usual — the truth is, I have been too full for
utterance. This has been to me a strangely sweet
day. I have had a peculiar feeling that my work is
done. While at prayer this morning I received an
assurance that my prayer for one for whom I have
prayed night and day since I was saved, would be
answered during these meetings. I want to say to-
night that no words can tell how I love the holiness
people, and how thankful I am for the holiness movement. You all know what I was, and I believe you
know I have what I profess when I say I am saved
and sanctified. Since I was sanctified it has been
my custom to ask in prayer every morning for a
text — a special text — for the day. One was given

me this morning that has strangely affected me all day. It was this: 'This day thou shalt be with me in paradise.'"

At that moment the electric light wire, by pre-arrangement, was cut, and the whole tent and encampment was in total darkness. The hoodlums yelled and turned loose a perfect sluice of eggs upon the people. The evangelist called loudly to the people to keep their seats and keep quiet, which they did. A number of men ran to their tents for lamps, and by the time Hess and his gang were off of the grounds the tent was well lighted up, and the people were singing lustily. When order was restored, it was found that the aim of the egg brigade had been too high, and they had thrown over the heads of the people.

Dr. Gall and Mr. Youngduck had sent Sister Dishrattler out to listen to the evangelist and report to them if he said anything against the "properly constituted authorities of the church." She was sitting just in front of the pulpit, note book and pencil in hand, when the excitement began. She leaped to her feet, and tore about in a great flurry, and was pelted with stale eggs in a most merciless manner. No one else was struck with an egg. As soon as Sister Dishrattler could be quieted and taken from the tent, the evangelist stood up to preach, and noticed that Happy John was lying full length on his face in the straw in front of the speaker's desk. He stepped down, and placing his hand upon him, gave him a gentle shake. Receiving no response, he turned him over, and to his astonishment found that happy John was dead.

CHAPTER XIV.

THY SIN WILL FIND THEE OUT.

The evangelist asked the people to sing, and beckoning a few friends to him, they took John up tenderly and carried him to one of the tents where he was placed upon a cot, and on examination they found that his skull had been crushed in just in front of, and a little above, his right ear. The evangelist went back to the altar, and looking in the straw, found, just where John's head lay, a scale's weight, marked 100, with a small piece broken out of one side, and lead run in the holes. The weight was stained with blood, and upon examination fitted exactly into the deep dent in John's skull. Two men were quietly sent away for the chief of police, and the meeting went forward as if nothing out of the regular order of things had occurred.

A number of souls were saved that night, and a strange awe rested upon the vast assembly. Sympathy for the holiness people was greatly intensified, and it was whispered about among thoughtful groups of men everywhere, "If it had not been for the bitter opposition of Dr. Gall and Mr. Youngduck, this shameful disturbance would not have occurred."

At the conclusion of the services, the evangelist announced to the people that Happy John was dead, that, during the attack of the mob, he had been struck on the head and killed. He also announced that John's funeral sermon would be preached at the camp-ground the next afternoon at three o'clock. He asked the people to be quiet, and to let nothing divert their minds from the great work in which they were engaged, to permit no feeling of revenge to rise up in their breasts, but to press the work for the salvation of souls as if nothing unusual had occurred.

Just before the onslaught at the big tent in which John was killed, Huton noticed Hess standing near the pulpit, and he also noticed that when lights were brought Hess had left, and was not seen on the grounds after the disturbance. Putting these facts together, he at once suspected Hess with being connected with the crime.

The two young men detailed by Hess to remain on the grounds, as soon as they heard that Happy John was dead, hurried to the rendezvous back of the barroom, where they found Hess and his gang drinking heavily. When they told the news of John's death, silence fell on the boisterous crowd, which, after a considerable pause, was broken by one of the most sober ones in the party who said, "Somebody threw something harder than an egg, and whoever did it ought to exonerate the boys by confessing up."

"Hess, where is that weight you put in **your**

pocket just as we started to the camp? " said another. "What do you mean? I've got no weight in my pocket," said Hess, "besides that, it is getting late and you boys must all get out of here." With that he cleared the room, took several drinks of whiskey, fell upon a couch and was soon in a deep sleep.

After the services closed at the camp-ground, Hicks and Huton went into town, and directed the chief of police to arrest Jack Hess, and two other suspicious characters who had been seen with him at the camp-ground. The three were lodged in jail before daylight Monday morning. Hess was so drunk that he hardly realized his situation; the two young men arrested with him confessed Monday morning that they were with the mob, and that Hess had placed the weight with which John was killed in his pocket on starting to the camp-ground. As Hess began to recover from his drunken stupor, he cried and begged the jailor not to let the mob have him.

Dr. Gall's first information of the unfortunate affair was on Monday morning. After coming down from his room, he was sitting in the parlor of Young-duck's boarding house waiting for breakfast. He was glancing over the morning paper and his eye fell on the following paragraph: "The shocking tragedy which took place at Huton's Camp-ground last night, a full account of which will be found else-where in this paper, is the culmination of the conflict which has been going on in religious circles for some months past in the city of Newton For years we have been laboring under the mistaken notion that this great country of ours was a land of such absolute religious liberty, that every man could worship according to the dictates of his conscience. under his own vine and fig tree, and none would dare molest or make him afraid. But recent developments reveal the fact that swaggering little ecclesiastics propose to dictate to their fellowmen when and how they shall worship. Had not certain preachers, whose ministry is only conspicuous because of its barrenness, been doing all in their power to oppose and hinder the meetings in Huton's woods, the disgraceful affair of last night never would have taken place. The party who killed happy John ought to be punished to the utmost limit of the law. Meanwhile public opinion will liberally lay the lash upon the men who have fomented the spirit of strife and hate that has culminated in murder. The disturbance of last night will only advertise the campmeeting. Thousands of people who had thought but little of the matter, will now sympathize with the holiness people. One would think that by this time the opposers of this great spiritual awakening would have learned to heed the advice of Gamaliel to the Jews concerning the apostles: 'Refrain from these men, and let them alone; for if this counsel or this work be of men, it will come to naught. But if it be of God, ye can not overthrow it; lest haply ye be found even to fight against God.'"

When Dr. Gall finished reading this editorial, the paper dropped from his hand and he sat in silence. Mr. Youngduck read the editorial and had nothing to say.

Dr. Gall had scarcely finished his breakfast when a boy rang the door bell, bringing the doctor a note from Hess, begging him to come at once to the jail. Hess, having slept off his drunkenness, was beginning to fully awake to the situation, and, like a drowning man catching at a straw, knowing that Dr. Gall was so bitterly opposed to the camp-meeting, he determined to send for him.

"What can I do about this?" said Dr. Gall to Mr. Youngduck.

"I hardly know what to say," he answered.

"You see from the morning paper that we are blamed for the trouble, and now this wretch of a barkeeper has sent for me. If I go down there it will make no end of talk," said Dr. Gall. Youngduck was of the same opinion. "Oh, will peace never come to the church again! This holiness movement has given me more trouble than any and all things put together; I wish now I had let the thing entirely alone," said the distressed ecclesiastic.

Poor Dr. Gall, how happily he might have been

engaged in the great work of salvation at the camp-meeting, if only he had been true to his ordination vows, and instead of fighting entire sanctification, had groaned after it, and come into its posession. Then, how the thousands of people at the camp in Huton's woods would have loved and rallied around him, and doubtless many scores from this very camp-meeting would have risen up in eternity to call him blessed. His chagrin and humiliation were all brought upon him by his own behaviour. What he had sown he must reap. Yet stupid and blind with prejudice, he really believed that the great revival was to blame for the uncomfortable position in which he found himself.

After a short council with Mr. Youngduck, Dr. Gall hurriedly packed his grip and left the city on the nine o'clock train, asking Youngduck to send a note to Hess stating that Dr. Gall was out of the city.

Dr. Gall went to the home of a married daughter, some fifty miles in the country, where he took some weeks of much needed rest, after the past few months of arduous toil and vexing care, amid the duties of his responsible office.

In all the history of Newton there never was seen so large a concourse of people as that which attended Happy John's funeral at the camp-ground at three o'clock Monday afternoon.

Huton was the speaker of the occasion. He was

possessed of a voice of remarkable volume, and the vast thousands listened with closest attention while Huton, in plain, simple language, preached them an earnest sermon on full salvation. Happy John lay in a casket, covered with flowers, on the platform just to the speaker's left. At the conclusion of the sermon, Huton pointed to the casket and called on the people to witness that "there lies a demonstration of the power of Christ to save to the uttermost." As the speaker referred to John's deep degradation, and the wonderful salvation that had been wrought in him, and of his last triumphant day on earth, and his tragic but glorious death, thousands of people were in tears, the altar was cleared, and the call for seekers given. Scores of people came seeking pardon or purity. The service continued until only time was left to take John's remains to the cemetery before dark, but as the procession drove away to the graveyard a number of struggling souls remained at the altar, with a company of faithful workers, refusing to be comforted until they were blessed.

When the grave in which John's body was laid away was filled up, and covered with the flowers, and the benediction pronounced, while the friends were pausing for a moment, there came hurrying through the crowd a man with bloated face, blood-shot eyes and matted hair, in tattered garments, who fell on his knees at the grave and wept as if his heart would break. The man was Whiskey Jim. It was a pathetic sight. Jim's fountain of tears had been sealed up for many a year, but finally his frozen heart had been thawed out, and the grief he felt at the loss of his last friend, as he thought, poured itself out in a perfect flood of tears. Huton motioned the crowd away, and remained alone with poor Jim until he could somewhat restrain his grief, then Huton dissuaded him from his purpose to spend the night in the cemetery at John's grave. He took Jim with him in his carriage to the city, gave him a bath, a hair cut, and a decent suit of clothes, and took him out to the camp-ground. Whiskey Jim was one of the first persons at the altar that night, and one of the first to be converted.

The next morning at six o'clock Jim stood with tears of gratitude coursing down his cheeks ringing the bell which called the people to the morning prayer service.

The camp-meeting went forward with accumulating power, and spreading in its influence over a wide territory of country. More than four hundred souls were either converted or sanctified during the meetings.

When Hess' examining trial came up, the fellow Karoon, with whom Hess talked so freely just before the tragedy, was a very damaging witness against him. He swore that he had heard Hess threaten to kill Happy John, and identified the weight with which John had been killed as the one Hess had in his possession just before the tragedy. Several other witnesses corroborated the testimony of Karoon, and Hess was committed to jail without bail.

Hicks and Huton volunteered their services to the district attorney, prepared the case for prosecution, and then persuaded Hess' lawyer to save his client's life by getting him to confess his crime, which he did in open court, and was sent to State's prison for life. Hess' confession was published in full in one of the city papers, and would make interesting reading if space would permit our publishing it in full. I will give only a brief paragraph:

" I was deeply impressed with the meetings at the store. I knew there was a power in them above human power. I thought seriously of seeking salvation myself, but when the two preachers, Mr. Gall and Mr. Youngduck, began to oppose the meetings, as I read their objections published in the papers, they seemed to destroy all the good resolutions that were forming in me, and seeing my old customers leaving me, my heart was filled with a great hatred against the holiness revivals, and I determined to join with the preachers and do all I could to break up such meetings. But for the opposition to the meetings on the part of the two preachers named,

I never would have committed the crime, and I believe I would to-day be a happy Christian man."

Huton held religious services in the jail, and did what he could to lead Hess to a better life, but the man seemed to be most all animal, with but little power to think of his soul or of the sin he had committed. He went away to the penitentiary with some hopeful signs of repentance, and a Bible which Huton gave him, with the promise that he would read it.

Mr. Youngduck went East to attend a Chatauqua, and make a run through New England.

The regular holiness prayer-meeting was held each week with a large attendance, and people were constantly converted and sanctified at these meetings.

From the camp-meeting, the revival fire had been carried to many communities, and was kindled in many homes and hearts.

Many of those who were wholly sanctified at the Huton camp-meeting on going home sought out the poor and destitute and told them of the great salvation, and so the good work went forward until scores of people who did not attend were brought into a gracious state of salvation. The good resulting from one of these great holiness camp-meetings can not possibly be estimated.

The effects of these meetings are especially

marked among the people of the humbler walks of life. There is a freedom of soul, an abandonment from all that stiffness that in our churches so often hinders the spirit of true worship, and the people worship with an enthusiasm and joy that is indeed refreshing.

CHAPTER XV.

THE CHURCH ENTERTAINMENT.

Sister Dishrattler was so completely unnerved by the excitement through which she passed at the camp-meeting, that she took to her bed, and for several days tried hard to believe she was sick. But she was a woman of indomitable spirit, and when she found that Dr. Gall and Mr. Youngduck had both fled the field, she determined to rally her forces and come to the rescue. For several days she quietly planned her enterprise and finally hit upon an idea.

Up to this time Sister Dishrattler had opposed holiness more from a general want of any information on the subject than anything else, but since her great humiliation at the camp-meeting, in which one of her best dresses was spoiled, she had become intensely bitter in her heart against the holiness people, and was set on going to opposite extremes in introducing all the worldliness into the church she possibly could. She had noticed that the dancers and theater goers in Central Church, had, with but few exceptions, united against the revival, and that had drawn her out to those people if possible even more than usual. She had promised the young people a big dance in her house early in the fall, but as quite a large number of the people in Central Church had professed sanctification, and she knew they would all object to a festival in the church, she was determined to have one of the most attractive entertainments ever given for the benefit of a church in Newton. Accordingly a company of young ladies were asked to meet at her house one afternoon, to arrange for a church entertainment. About thirty young ladies responded to the call. Most of them had joined the church during a *card-signing* protracted meeting.

Mr. Youngduck had supplied them with a number of anti-holiness books, and they were fully satisfied with the subject as discussed and settled by the writer of these books; there being nothing in them to arouse the conscience of an unconverted church member. Their religion consisted in making fun of the holiness people, and assisting at church festivals.

If a serious person undertook to warn or instruct them on the subject, they would say, "The bishops and leading men of our church are against it," and dismiss the subject with the utmost disdain.

A few days after the meeting of the young ladies at Sister Dishrattler's, the following notice appeared in one of the daily papers of Newton:

"SOMETHING NEW."

"An entertainment will be given at Central Methodist Church in this city on next Friday evening, by the young ladies of that church, their young lady friends of other churches assisting them, which promises to surpass in novelty anything ever offered for public entertainment by the church people of Newton. First of all there will be given a broom drill by a select band of Newton's most attractive beauties, in short skirts. Next, 'Josiah Allen's Wife' will be rendered by the young people, who have been selected and trained by Prof. Backus, of Boston, well known as a successful trainer for church concerts. A large stage, with scenery, and a drop curtain has been arranged, so that this remarkably funny comedy may be rendered to the best possible advantage.

"The entertainment will be closed with an 'old time back country husking bee,' which will doubtless be the most laughable thing on the entire program.

"A load of genuine corn in the husk will be placed on the stage, and divided into two equal heaps, then two young fellows in shirt sleeves, and one gallus, will choose up. The girls will be dressed to appear as blooming country lasses. There will be ten persons on each side, and the race will be an exciting one. The party that gets through first will be rewarded with an immense cake, said to be the largest ever baked in Newton. The most interesting feature about the husking bee is the fact that any boy finding a red ear of corn is entitled to kiss the girl opposite him at the corn heap. It is said that a party of young men went out from Newton yesterday in the country and offered some farm laborers ten cents each for all the unhusked ears of red corn that they will deliver them before eight o'clock Friday evening.

"It is to be hoped that the zeal and enterprise

of the good women who have labored so faithfully to make a success of this entertainment will be rewarded with a large and appreciative audience."

Huton and Hicks did all in their power to keep this disgraceful affair out of the church, but without avail.

The committee of women who had charge of the entertainment wrote to Dr. Gall, asking for the use of the church, and he wrote them that he had no objections whatever. This entertainment drew the lines closely between the holiness and the anti-holiness elements in the church.

The holiness people could not conscientiously take part in the entertainment, or attend it. This seemed only to increase the enthusiasm of those who opposed holiness, and many remarks were made, of which the following is a fair sample: "Well, if this sanctification disqualifies people for a little innocent enjoyment, it certainly is not from heaven. Why, heaven itself is a place of enjoyment. Just look at all nature; the very birds and fish and insects are happy. I believe in laughter and merriment myself. The time will come soon enough when we shall all have to weep, that will be time enough to put on a long face," said the society sister, with a literary turn of mind, in low neck and short sleeves.

"If we all got sanctified, I would like to know who would keep up the church," said the strutting little politician, who had not given five dollars to the church in seven years. The only way to get money out of his pocket for the church was with ice cream, or strawberries, or some sort of a church concert.

The absence of the holiness people at the entertainment, brought forth the remark from Sister Dishrattler that Dr. Gall had told them that *come-out-ism* would be sure to follow the store and camp-meetings.

"Well," said Hicks to Huton, as they sat in their office on the evening of the entertainment, "First and last I have put into Central Church more than fifteen hundred dollars. Dr. Gall has never put a nickle into it, yet he can shut us out from the basement when we want to read Wesley's Sermons to the people, and try to get them saved, and then he can, over our protest, turn in this show, and a mass of people who really have no intelligent Christian love for the church, and who contribute nothing in a substantial way to its support. It seems to me that this is a most deplorable state of things."

"Take care of your loyalty, my brother, you should submit meekly when the properly constituted authorities of the church have spoken," said Huton with a sad smile.

After a long, thoughtful pause, Hicks said, "Do you know that while Methodism has been the most spiritual church, and I may say a church in which preachers and people enjoyed the largest liberty along all lines of worship and work for the salvation of men, it appears to me now that we are quite likely to become the most worldly, and, at the same time, the most priest-ridden church in the land? The tendency is to swing to the opposite extreme from original Methodism. Doctrine is neglected, and *law* is magnified, but it is plain that church discipline, which is for the regulation of the behavior, and the development of the Christian character, is almost a dead letter, and the cry of 'law' and 'loyalty' simply means that the opposers of the great doctrines of our church, do not intend that the people shall have an opportunity to hear the gospel of full salvation preached, at least it is their purpose to do their utmost to prevent their having it preached."

HUTON: "The truth is, Brother Hicks, we have been having an easy time in this country. We need something to develop Christian courage and character, and while there are some very sad features about all this opposition to the great revival, there is a bright side to it also. I am not a prophet, and have not been long enough identified with the holiness movement to even guess at what the future has in store for us, but we all know that history repeats itself. A kite rises against the wind, you know. All we have to do is to be true to God. Everything else will take care of itself. I am not much concerned for the future, only I know that the same power which opened the Red Sea, and made the Jordan to stand on heaps while Israel passed over dry shod, is mighty to save to the uttermost, and to lead in safety all who will follow Him. Our part is to follow, and not to go ahead of Him. There is one thing certain: God is in this movement, and the devil hates it. Of these facts there can be no doubt. Whereunto it will grow no man can tell. I believe, however, that our church will suffer irreparable loss because of the opposition to the revival. Take this affair at the church to-night, for example. These poor, deluded people are going to fearful extremes to show their contempt for the views and wishes of the holiness people. At least that is manifestly an element in the affair.

"The truth is, Brother Hicks, the doctrine of entire sanctification is the doctrine of the Holy Ghost. The Holy Ghost purifies the heart, and to reject the doctrine and experience of entire sanctification is to reject the Holy Ghost. Just as the Jews rejected the second person of the trinity, thousands of our Methodist people are rejecting the third person of the trinity. It is a fearful thought, but it is undoubtedly true. And there is no more hope for the salvation of a Gentile who rejects the Holy Spirit, than there is for the Jew who rejects

Jesus. Just as the Jews who rejected Jesus drifted away from God the Father, so will the Gentiles who reject the Holy Ghost drift away from God the Son. I sometimes think we are approaching a crisis in human history. You know when the Jewish Church rejected Christ. God overthrew and scattered His chosen people. What are we to expect when the Christian Church rejects the Holy Ghost?"

HICKS: "These are interesting and serious subjects to think on."

The two lawyers at this point separated for the night, and, if the reader would like, we will look in on the church entertainment for a few minutes.

The main auditorium is packed with a great throng of people. A large stage covers the organ platform and altar rail. Curtains cut off the alcove back of the pulpit for a dressing room. Twenty-five girls in skirts that come to their knees, and each with one white and one red stocking on, carries a broom. They are drilling now. The Boston professor is in uniform, with a sword belted about him. He has trained them carefully, and they perform so well that the audience, so much opposed to excitement and shouting in holiness meetings, cheers them lustily time after time.

Now we have Josiah Allen, wife and boy, with first and last a score of other actors on the stage.

The performance of this part of the program

lasts an hour. To persons who have no thought of where they are, and no reverence for, or fear of God, no doubt it is laughable. But to thoughtful Christian people it is a horrible scene. Theaters full, dance-houses full, barrooms full, all on their way to eternal night, and now alas! alas! the church of God turned into a play house to amuse, with low, coarse play, a godless multitude.

Last of all came the corn husking. The young men had secured large quantities of red ears, and there was a constant scuffle with the girls for a kiss. The excitement became intense. Corn was kicked into the aisles, the struggling parties on the platform would step upon the rolling ears and fall to the floor.

The congregation was on its feet, shouting, cheering, amid roaring laughter. At ten o'clock the announcement was made that the ladies would serve refreshments in the basement room of the church, and while many of the people went to their homes, a large number went down into the basement to eat ice cream, popcorn, candy, and nuts. A grab-bag was rigged up near the door and each one, as he left, was asked to pay a nickle and try his luck.

But for a conversation which took place between two young men after they returned to their room that night, I would close this chapter here, but I think the reader will be interested in what follows, and although in much need of rest, and writing at a late hour, I will give the conversation as it came to me.

Harold Wilks and Henry Garth were neither of them members of the church, but were bright young men of the world. Wilks was a clerk for the gas company of Newton, and Garth was head clerk of a large dry goods establishment.

Unfortunately Garth had read many skeptical books, and was far from being orthodox in his beliefs and opinions.

"What do you think of such church entertainments as the one we have attended to-night," said Wilks.

GARTH: "Well, sir, do you know such scenes make me sad. You are aware that I have had certain doubts to contend with; well, when I look on scenes in the church of God like we have attended to-night, it strengthens my doubts."

WILKS: "I see how that could be. A man will naturally ask himself how true believers in Christ can stoop to such heathenish business."

GARTH: "Yes, I should have been disgusted with that show to-night if it had been given in a low theater, much less a church. Those people never have an entertainment of any kind that they do not come to me to buy a ticket, and to-night they were harassing me to buy popcorn and try my fortune in the grab-bag. I suppose there were not less than three hundred professed Christians there to-night, and they were after me for a nickle for this and that, but not a word about my soul. Now, according to their notion, they are all Christians and I am a sinner. If a cyclone had come along to-night and knocked that church over, those girls, in short skirts and variegated stockings, and that crowd around the corn pile, would have gone straight to heaven, but ah, poor me! Now, if that is what you call Christianity, I don't want it."

WILKS: "Well, Garth, you know that is not Christianity. I know it is not, and so do they know it is not. Real Christianity is love, love that gives, and gladly sacrifices all, and suffers cheerfully for Christ's sake."

GARTH: "Well, these people all know that I'm not a Christian, and they are always after my money, and not one of them has ever intimated to me that I have a soul. Do you know, this church that gave the entertainment to-night is the one that refused to let the holiness people hold their meeting in the basement rooms. I could not help thinking of that to-night. Old Mrs. Dishrattler and her crowd have just about ruined that church. By the way, she is to give a big ball in her house soon.

"But, it is late and I must go to sleep. All I have to say is, if I ever should get religion, I do not want the kind we have seen manifested to-night. People claiming to be saved, and yet strive to get a man's nickles and utterly neglect his soul! Good-night."

The reader will remember that Huton, in the beginning of this story, reminded Dr. Poolkins that he (Huton) had been elected delegate to the Annual Conference. The next chapter will give some account of the exciting incidents which took place at the Conference.

CHAPTER XVI.

THE ANNUAL CONFERENCE.

Unfortunately, the Bishop who held the Annual Conference this fall, in which Central Church was located, arrived in the State several days before the meeting of the conference, and stopped for those days in the home of Dr. Gall. The doctor poured into the bishop's ear a flood of talk about the fanaticism and insubordination that had been brought into his district by the advent of the holiness movement. And while we do not believe the man really intended to misrepresent the facts, there was hardly a sentence of clean, winnowed truth in all of his statements.

Fanaticism there had been none. And the only disturbance that had existed had been produced, not by preaching the Methodist doctrine of entire sanctification, but by opposition to this doctrine by Methodist preachers who themselves ought to have been preaching it.

The bishop heard Dr. Gall with great interest, and determined to administer a castigation to the holiness people at the conference, which, he believed, would put a decided check upon its progress.

At the appointed day the conference met. Preachers, lay delegates, and visiting friends were on the ground in full force. Huton was present to represent his district, and Hicks had come along to enjoy the occasion.

A large group of preachers were gathered before the church doors before the hour for the morning prayer-meeting, and there was much good fellowship among them. They loved one another, and had a most peculiar love and affection for their bishop. Whatever difference of opinion may have existed among them on points of doctrine, there was between them that strong bond of common interest and sympathy that binds Methodist preachers into one of the closest and most sacred unions that exist between men on this earth of ours.

The preachers were looking well and happy, and the opening hymn of the conference was sung with great warmth and fervor. The tears coursed their way down the face of many battle-scarred soldiers of the cross, as from their heart they thanked God that they were "yet alive, and saw each other's face."

The prayer was offered by an old veteran of loving heart, and was unctious.

When the bishop stood up to read the lesson there was in the whole conference a spirit of love, union, and prayer that made a soil peculiarly ready to receive any good seed the bishop might see fit to cast in. But, alas! alas! The bishop stood up to read. He was a man of striking appearance, well

proportioned physically, with good head, and clean.
clear, strong face. I regret to say there was a
strong odor of tobacco that enveloped him, which
was painfully perceptible to all who sat to windward
of the dignified figure.

The whole manner of the man was autocratic.
Consciousness of authority sat upon his brow, har-
dened his lips, and looked keenly out from his eyes.
The lesson selected was the second chapter of 1st
John. The bishop read and commented. The hearts
of the brethren glowed under his words. There was
a feeling of relief, and hope among the preachers.
With the exception of a small number of men, who
were very bitter against the holiness movement,
there was in the conference a general desire that the
subject of entire sanctification might be permitted
to rest. It was a well known fact among the preacn-
ers that the doctrine of the second work of grace was
the doctrine of the church. If some of the brethren
believed it, and desired to preach it, no one had a
right to say them nay, and the preachers generally
had grown tired of having their brethren getting
their annual castigation from the bishop, whom they
all knew had himself promised to "groan after it."

The tenth verse was reached, "He that loveth his
brother abideth in the light." "I believe in love,"
said the bishop, "but I do not believe in a man having so much love that he thinks he is so much better

than other people, that he will cross the street to keep from shaking hands with a brother."

The bishop's eyes flashed, and with clinched fist he said, "One of that kind told a lie on me; yes, put it in his paper when he knew it was a lie, and when he did that he lost his second blessing." He looked around with a twinkle in his eye, as much as to say, "I guess that will put the breaks on your holiness movement."

A few very small men blandly smiled their approval. Like the "ass" that "knoweth his master's crib," they had trained themselves to approve all that came from the lips of a chief pastor. Not so with the conference. It was made up of a body of strong, manly, Christian men. They could hardly believe their own eyes and ears. Were they looking upon and listening to a Methodist Bishop? Would the man dare to get up before a conference of Methodist preachers and thus go out of his way to rake up some personal matter, and call a man a liar, who was at the moment not less than five hundred miles away, in order to slap at the doctrine of entire sanctification, the doctrine of the baptism of the Holy Ghost?

In the State in which the conference was being held, men had grown up to regard the giving of the lie equal to the striking of a blow, and they were not willing that even a bishop should stand up in a

Methodist pulpit and call an absent brother a liar, even though it gave him an opportunity to insinuate that the people who professed the second blessing were hypocrites. The sanctified preachers looked with pity and sorrow on the poor man. There was not one of them who felt in the least terrified, or who would at that moment have hesitated to testify to the cleansing power of the blood of Jesus.

The opposers said that their champion had overshot the mark, and that the reflex action, resulting from his sarcasm, would create sympathy for the holiness people.

A large body of conservative, good men, who were not especially identified with the holiness movement or against it, were disgusted. One of the best men of the conference said to the writer, "For the first time in my life I was ashamed of a Methodist Bishop."

The ten minute speech of the bishop had done great harm to the cause of Christ. The good feeling that had characterized the conference when he arose had been swept away, the chasm had been widened between the two elements in the church, and the attention of all visitors from other denominations had been called to the fact that there is an unpleasant condition of things in the Methodist family. During the whole morning the conference could not shake off the evil effect of the opening speech.

The bishop's remarks effectually cut him off from

all of those men of the conference who held on to the old Methodist doctrine, and drew closer to him a body of men, who were not only un-Methodistic in doctrine and practice, but men who were eager to see enacted unjust laws that would in the end change Methodism from a glorious evangelism to a stilted, narrow, arrogant ecclesiasticism.

We shall not undertake to follow in detail the workings of the conference, but will give the reader some items of interest.

The second morning of the conference, the hour from eight to nine having been appointed for devotional meetings, the sanctified people were out in large numbers. The singing was lively, prayers earnest, and testimonies quick and to the point. Most all who testified were rejoicing in the sanctifying power of Jesus' blood.

The next morning a strong anti-holiness brother had charge of the meeting. After reading the lesson, the brother said, "Now, brethren, we ought to devote this hour, not to testimony and song, but to prayer." The people all understood that this move was made to cut off the holiness songs, and testimonies, but it was nothing new, and they submitted cheerfully.

The first item of special interest was the offering of a resolution by Dr. Gall condemning all so-called holiness camp-meetings, and demanding that all

members of the Methodist Church, South, both clerical and lay, desist from holding, or attending such
meetings.

An animated discussion followed. Dr. Gall made
a speech in which he stated that the continuance of
these meetings meant that the entire church would
become honey-combed with the second blessing heresy, and general insubordination and disobedience to
"the regularly constituted authorities of the church."
"Already," said he, "there is rising up among us
a class of aggressive Methodists who do not hesitate
to say openly that the office of presiding elder is a
fifth wheel, a useless and expensive appendage to
our Methodism. Yes, Bishop, these holiness people
have convictions, and a daring in expressing themselves that is absolutely startling. Why, sir, let
this so-called revival spread throughout Southern
Methodism, and the views and teachings of Wesley,
Clark, and Fletcher become thoroughly disseminated
among the people, and men like you and myself
would actually be unacceptable in the church, turned
out like an old, useless horse to graze, to pick up our
living as best we could amid the decrepitudes of our
old age."

The bishop was manifestly embarrassed, the anti-
holiness people hung their heads. Meanwhile the
Wesleyan element in the conference were well
pleased, and anxious for Dr. Gall to proceed. The

doctor became conscious that something was wrong, grew red in the face, and began to try to make a landing. "So far as the camp-meetings are concerned," said the doctor, "I have no objections to the people gathering in the woods for a few days' meeting, but the trouble is we can't control these meetings. Evangelists and preaching laymen come to these meetings, who are not under our thumb, they are not dependent upon us for their bread, the people love them and have confidence in them, and are taught by them that Wesley and the fathers and founders of Methodism taught and experienced this blessing. Why, sir, they are flooding the country with the old Methodist biographies and books. What are we to do? We can shut them out of our churches, but what does this amount to when they can fill the woods with these holiness camp-meetings, and get the people converted and sanctified in spite of us? And, Bishop, if we fill up the church with people converted at these camp-meetings, under the ministry of these sanctified preachers, I tell you they will be praying and seeking for this second blessing in spite of all we can do. Our only hope of stamping out this old Methodist doctrine is to stamp out the holiness camp-meetings."

The situation became unbearable. The bishop smote the table in front of him with the gavel in his hand with a force that made several of the brethren start from their seats. "I think you have said enough, brother," said the bishop, and poor Dr. Gall stood trembling with emotion: his face was red with excitement, and streaming with perspiration.

Poor man! For forty years he had been soaking himself with tobacco juice, and the sad effects were beginning to manifest themselves.

The doctor had not said what he intended to say at all, but he had said what he had been *thinking* for some months past, and thinking so strongly, that, out of the abundance of his heart, his mouth, in the excitement of the moment, had spoken He dropped into his seat a crest-fallen man, and there was something in the face of the bishop that showed to those who can spell out the meaning of the expressions of a man's face, that Dr. Gall would be presiding elder no longer. And so it was.

During the awkward pause that followed Dr. Gall's discomfiture, Huton arose and said: "Mr. Chairman, I object to this resolution. I shall not take up the time of the conference with a lengthy speech, but will be perfectly frank in the remarks that I shall make. The holiness camp-meeting has grown out of a condition of things that to my mind is sad to contemplate. There is not an honest man of moderate research and information in this body who will deny that the doctrine of entire sanctification as a second work of grace is a doctrine of the Methodist Church.

The men who, under God, brought forth Methodism in the travail of their great, ardent souls, believed and taught this doctrine and left it a precious heritage to us, their spiritual sons.

"Many of our ministers, notwithstanding their pledges at the bar of the conference, have ceased to groan after or to preach this soul-searching truth of cleansing from all sin.

"The holiness camp-meeting has grown up out of the hungry condition of multitudes of starving souls, who have looked to recreant ministers for bread, and received stones. The churches, sir, which we have built with our own money, and dedicated to God, have had their doors shut in our faces, when we would meet in them to inquire for the old Methodist faith, and seek those enduements of power that made our fathers such dauntless heroes of the cross, and those same doors which have been shut in our faces, have been thrown wide open to admit the world with entertainments unfit for theaters, much less the house of God. Meanwhile the fires of devotion have burned low, and, sad to say, have gone out upon many of our family altars, while our unsaved children have gone astray from the fold of Christ. These very rooms in our sanctuary, once dedicated to testimony and praise, are now polluted with cake-walks and feasts of the flesh. What are we to do? How can we sit still?

"We have turned in our distress to God's first temples, and, under the spreading, friendly trees, have cried to God for a revival of religion, and, thank God, it has come. Vast thousands of souls have been saved at the improvised altars in the holiness camp-meetings.

"Did we forsake our church, or cease to render financial support to the very men who refused to permit us to seek at her altars the experiences taught in her doctrinal standards, and the course of study prescribed by our chief pastors?

"No, sir; we have remained true to our church, and to every vow we ever took at her sacred altars. But the opposers of her doctrine, the destroyers of her peace, and the wasters of her heritage have followed us to the woods with their persecutions. They refuse us the privilege of assembling together, and bowing down at the roots of the trees in our own woodland pastures, and of praying God to grant us the baptism of the Holy Ghost in his sanctifying power.

"Who is doing all this? Is it our laymen? Is it the men whose money builds our churches, erects our colleges, sends abroad our missionaries, and supports our ministry? No, sir; it is not.

"Then who is it that says we shall not seek entire sanctification in our churches, or assemble in our cottages to pray for, read, and talk about this grace?

Yes, sir, propose to close the sacred precincts of our own doors, and refuse us liberty to pray with a company of neighbors at our own hearthstones? Who so arrogant at the dawn of the new century, in enlightened and liberty-loving America, as thus to hunt us down in the very woods, break up our meetings, and interfere with our religious rights? Who is it. I ask?"

Huton swept his hand over the audience, and his voice thundered out the question so loud that the church fairly trembled. The excitement was intense. A number of men were on their feet in a moment. "I object to such a speech being made upon this conference floor," said a number of voices at once. As many more cried out, "Go on, go on." "Mr. Chairman," cried half a dozen. Not less than a dozen of the leading Methodist laymen of the State were present, and gathered about the bishop, saying, "Bishop, Brother Huton must be permitted to make his speech, if he is not, we will withdraw from the conference room in a body." Huton stood calmly waiting until the excitement had subsided and quiet was restored. His face was as calm as if he were strolling across his yard on a May morning.

"We have had considerable excitement," said our speaker with a smile, "but no one has answered my question; then I shall answer it myself, It is *Methodist preachers.* Men who have eaten at our tables, slept upon our beds, and been supported by our hard-earned dollars   They are the men, sir, who propose to interfere with our religious liberties, and either force us to give up the doctrines of the Methodist Church. or else drive us from the membership of the church.

"Bishop, I stand here in my place to say that these brethren who have this enterprise in hand, have but little conception of the enormity of the task which they have undertaken to perform.   Let me assure you that we laymen are as far from desiring a state of anarchy in the church as any of our brethren.   We know the importance of law, and we not only intend to abide by the law, but we propose to enforce the law also.

"That there is a state of anarchy in the Methodist Church is a well-known fact, but it is not among the people known as the holiness people.

"Take the tens of thousands of our members who dance, play cards, attend theaters, and make sport of the second blessing,—do they recognize any law? Are they of the truly loyal?   No doubt they are free from aiding and abetting in holiness camp-meetings, but can the church control these people?   Do they not walk rough shod over law and order? and yet it seems to me that they and a certain class of our preachers, who have much to say about law and order, are on remarkably good terms.   I want to suggest to some one of Dr. Gall's friends to table this resolution. We do not intend to have this sort of thing in this conference, and we are fully prepared for the worst when it comes. The day for ecclesiastical tyranny and bossism is past in this country. We do not intend to leave the Methodist Church or be put out of it, nor be tyrannized over in it. We want peace, and propose to have it at any cost, except the sacrifice of conscience and religious liberty. If necessary, we will go with the opposers of this movement into an agitation of this question that will stir our church from center to circumference, and once the great heart and conscience of Methodism is aroused, woe be to that class of dictatorial men who have arisen among us, prating about *loyalty*, and proposing to shackle and fetter the consciences of their fellow men." As Huton took his seat. a perfect volley of amens, repeated again and again. swept over the audience.

CHAPTER XVII.

IN CHARGE OF A MISSION.

When the noise of the amens and cheers which followed Huton's speech died away sufficiently for a voice to be heard, "I move you that we table the resolution," said a preacher. The motion was seconded, and the resolution tabled without a dissenting voice.

Huton's speech had produced a most marvelous effect upon the conference. Weak men became strong and courageous. Laymen, on the streets, in the homes of the people, and about the church doors, spoke out plainly in favor of law, but with no uncertain sound against ecclesiastical tyranny.

The conservative element of the preachers said the time had come when all of this unwarranted and silly persecution of the holiness people, and ridicule of the doctrines of Methodism in the Methodist Church, must stop. But one of the most startling incidents of the conference was Mr. Youngduck's failure to be received on trial, in the traveling connection.

It came about in this way: When Mr. Youngduck's name was offered for admission on trial, and the preliminary steps had been taken, Dr. Searching took the floor and said:

"'This young brother comes to us recommended

by the district conference, and we are told that he is a graduate of Vanderbilt University, also that he has taken the theological course at that institution of learning. Very good. But there is this question I should like to ask before I vote for his admission into the conference. *Is he a Methodist preacher?*

"There are many preachers of the gospel who are men of God, of solid sense, and deep piety, who are not *Methodist preachers.* They belong to some other denomination. This is quite proper. Men in the Methodist ministry ought to be Methodist preachers. We have our peculiar doctrines, and discipline, and we want men in our conference who will preach our doctrines and enforce our discipline. When I speak of the enforcement of discipline, I do not mean that we want men to strain a point of law in order to drive from our church a few humble people who believe and profess the original doctrines and experiences of Methodism, but I mean a man who will purge the church of the worldliness that has swept in upon us.

"The times demand Methodist preachers for the Methodist Church. Men of deep convictions and dauntless courage, who will not pander to popular notions, or be led away by new theories of doctrine. Men full of faith and the Holy Ghost, who, in the pulpit and out of it, will impress upon the people everywhere, and all the time, that great and neg-

.ected Bible truth, that, '*without holiness no man shall see the Lord.*' The only way to restore to our church peace and unity, purity and power, is to purge our pulpits of un-Methodistic men and teachings, and give our people '*sound doctrine.*'

"Is our brother Youngduck such a man? I regret to say, he is not. If any one will call in question my statements with regard to this young man, I am prepared to give proof of the correctness of them that will leave no room for doubt."

Dr. Searching took his seat. Dr Searching was a man of more influence perhaps than any other man in the conference. For the past eight years he had been presiding elder of two of the most important districts in his conference. He was a powerful preacher, and of true piety. He moved among his people like a true shepherd among his flocks. He was as an elder brother to the older preachers, and as a father to the younger ones in his district. His visits to the churches meant great congregations, and times of spiritual refreshing Good men loved him, and bad men feared him.

His districts were in a constant state of revival. He was a revivalist himself, and he had had one of the strongest evangelists at the largest towns on his districts, and some of the zealous young beginners at the villages and school houses along the isolated borders.

Dr. Searching was a kindly man in manner and spirit, but a fearless and strong man in debate. He was from top to toe a Methodist preacher, tried and true, and an ideal presiding elder. No one arose to answer his remarks with reference to Youngduck. After a considerable pause, a layman by the name of John Marshall, an influential and devout man, arose and said: "Bishop, as no one seems anxious to speak, I wish to offer a few remarks, and I feel quite sure that in what I shall say I represent most, if not all, of the laymen on this floor. I know all of the laymen here and have talked freely with them. We laymen are in the Methodist Church because we are *Methodists*, and we want *Methodist* preachers for our pastors. We are by no means ready to give up the old ship, although we are painfully conscious that there are breakers ahead. But we believe that with genuine *Methodist* preachers to man the craft, she can be brought safely into the open sea. We are not willing to have men of new-fangled notions and far-fetched theories teach our children, and corrupt our churches with strange fire upon Methodist altars.

"We are not willing to support such men with our money, or turn them loose in our families to lead them astray from the great Bible doctrines, the preaching of which brought us into existence as a separate body of Christians. We want Wesleyan

Methodist preachers, and we are not willing that any other kind shall be forced upon us

"Are we to be expected to support men who rob us of our birthright. and then, with strange doctrines in our pulpits, and our church doors shut in our faces, if we go to the woods to worship God as *Methodists*, be hounded there with threats of being turned out of the church, robbed of the supper of our Lord while we live, and of Christian burial when we die ? Brethren of the ministry, if ever there was a time when you should guard carefully the doors of this conference, that no enemy be permitted to enter our camp. now is the time."

Brother Marshall took his seat, and after a hurried consultation between Dr. Gall and a few of his friends. Dr. Gall begged leave of the conference to withdraw the name of Brother Youngduck. What finally became of the young man I do not know. The last I saw of him was some years since when traveling by private conveyance in the South. We had to cross a river in a ferryboat. Just as the ferryman was about to pull off from the shore, a man came driving up hurriedly, calling out to the boatman to wait for him. As he drove into the boat I looked up and saw that the new comer was seated in a no-top wagon, with an old sewing machine sitting behind the seat. As he drove out of the boat. the old machine tipped over and fell out of the wagon, and was considerably damaged by the mishap. I assisted the man to lift his machine back into the wagon, and being thus brought face to face with him, I thought I recognized him, and said, "Is not your name Youngduck?" He said, "It is."

I have not seen or heard of him from that day to this.

The conference closed without further incident that would interest the reader, except that Huton preached in the opera house Sabbath afternoon, at three o'clock, to a vast assembly of people, and quite a number of souls were converted and sanctified.

On the whole, the session closed a great victory for true Methodism. Preachers and laymen went to their homes with a self-respect and satisfaction they had not felt for years. They now knew, as they had not known before, that the opposers of the doctrines of the church are not so resolute and courageous as one would suppose; but when met with a bold and determined front, one true Methodist can chase a thousand of them, and two can put ten thousand to flight.

The reader will be pleased to know that Dr. Searching was made presiding elder of Newton district, and that Rev. Mr. Grace was stationed at Central Church. Grace was an excellent preacher, and a man of great strength of character. He had been in the experience of entire sanctification for

many years, and was a broad, true man, capable of
ministering wisely to the spiritual needs of all the
people of his charge. Under his ministry Sister
Dishrattler soon disappeared from leadership, and
a few of the most worldly and wicked of the members
of Central Church went away and joined the Episcopalians, but the great majority of the people—nine
tenths of them—were drawn away from worldliness
and sin, many of them converted, many reclaimed
from backsliding, and scores of them sanctified, and
in this way the church became a great power for
good in Newton. Out from it went ministers, teach-
ers, and missionaries, and by the time Grace closed
out his fourth year there was not a dancer, theater
goer, or card player left in the congregation, nor
had there been a church trial or expulsion. They
had either sought salvation or disappeared. At the
district conference following the coming of Dr.
Searching to the Newton District, Huton was licensed
to preach, and at his request was made a supply on
the poorest mission in the district. He gave up his
law practice entirely, and devoted his time to his
mission. He held meetings in schoolhouses, millsheds,
and brush arbors all over his charge, built two new
churches, a parsonage, and saw not less than five
hundred people converted or sanctified. The people
of Central Church took great interest in Huton's
mission, and the good people of all denominations in

Newton helped liberally in building the churches and parsonage. The following year the mission was raised to a circuit and an excellent young man sent by the conference to travel it. At the earnest solicitation of the leading laymen of a number of the largest cities of the South and West, Huton, during the year, left his mission for a six weeks tour of lectures on, "*Entire Sanctification* as taught by the Methodist Church," and "Entire Sanctification as taught in the Scriptures." He would speak twice, two evenings in each place he visited; the first evening he discussed the subject from a Methodist standpoint, and the second evening from a Bible point of view

He was met everywnere with large and enthusiastic audiences. Where the churches were large enough, he spoke in the churches, and where they would not accommodate the people, he spoke in halls.

At every point he visited, Methodism and Bible truth received a mighty impetus. When it was possible he would remain a few days, and preach full salvation to the people.

He met with several little protests against his coming, as he went on his way, but did not in a single instance either heed or answer them. He knew that the laity had reached a point of righteous indignation against little ecclesiastical tyrants, and that it would be better for the peace of the church if it was not known that these brethren had written him not to come to this or that city. In Dallas, Houston, and Waco, Texas; and at New Orleans, Birmingham, Chattanooga, Nashville, Knoxville, Atlanta, and Richmond, Virginia, and Washington City the better class of the preachers, as well as all classes of laymen, gave him a most cordial reception. Huton had many calls to hold protracted meetings, but refused them all, except when he had a few days between lectures. He traveled with Methodist standards, histories, and biographies in his grip, and read and digested them thoroughly, thus growing in head and heart as he went.

The following conference Huton was received on trial, and although a number of large stations were eager to have him for their pastor, he insisted on having a circuit, to which he was appointed. During the year a great revival swept over his circuit, and he also assisted in several revival meetings in various stations, where his labors were greatly blessed.

The following conference Huton was appointed to a large station, which he filled with great acceptability and success. During the year he also delivered his two now famous lectures in many of the leading Methodist churches in the large cities of the South He also took up his pen and wrote with great vigor

and clearness, both on the doctrines and government of the church.

Huton had now served on a mission, circuit, and
station, and at the close of his fourth year in the
last named charge he was made presiding elder of a
district, and elected on the first ballot a clerical
delegate to the coming General Conference. Dr.
Searching and Rev. Mr. Grace, pastor of Central
Church, were elected with him. Huton was chair
man of his delegation.

The General Conference was looked forward to
with great interest. The opposers of the holiness
movement and the Wesleyan doctrine of entire
sanctification were marshaling their hosts for a final
and determined effort to capture the offices of the
church, and enact laws so rigid and unreasonable
that they would be able to drive from the church all
of those who would not in meekness bow to their
tyrannical dictation.

It was at this conference, as the reader shall see,
that Huton rendered his church a most valuable
service, and turned the tide of battle for Methodism,
in its purity and simplicity, for Christ and humanity.

CHAPTER XVIII.

ENFORCING THE LAW.

During the four years that Dr. Searching was presiding elder of the Newton District, and Mr. Grace was minister in charge at Central Church, the Huton Camp-ground became a great center of religious influence and power. The people came to this camp-meeting from all over the conference, and many were saved and sanctified.

There was only one presiding elder left in the conference who was especially bitter in his opposition to the holiness movement; he had gathered about him in his district several congenial spirits, among them a brother by the name of Wrong — Rev. W. A. Wrong. This brother had charge of a small station, and, in addition to his work as pastor, he published a little eight-page monthly, which he called the *Vesuvius*, in the columns of which he delighted to abuse and misrepresent the holiness people. In Brother Wrong's charge there was a man by the name of Wright, who was a successful business man, and although a steward in the church, he was strongly inclined to worldliness.

He was quite liberal with his money, always ready to entertain a preacher, and prompt to attend church on Sabbath *mornings*, but that was about the extent of his religion. He would attend the theaters, take his children to the circus, and give card parties and dances in his house. The town in which Mr. Wright lived being only about fifty miles from Newton. Mr. Wright determined to take his family down and spend a few days at the Huton holiness camp-meeting. He went out of the merest curiosity, to see the crowd, and to meet with friends who had promised to be present.

But it was with Wright, as it has been with many others who went to laugh, and remained to pray. He had not been on the ground twenty-four hours until he was most powerfully converted. His wife and oldest child soon followed him into the kingdom, and a few days later they all entered Canaan land together. Wright was impatient to get home and tell Brother Wrong what a glorious change had come to him, and felt quite sure that his pastor would let him send for an evangelist and hold a meeting in their church, which had not known a good revival for more than fifteen years. When he reached home he went at once to the parsonage and told his pastor of the wonderful meeting at the camp-ground, and how that he himself had been both converted and sanctified. To his surprise, Brother Wrong said but little, and looked quite displeased.

At the suggestion of a revival, Wrong gave him

to understand that he was the pastor of the church, and would hold meetings when it suited him to do so.

"Well," said Mr. Wright. "if you do not object, we will have a little prayer meeting in one of the basement rooms of the church on Friday evenings; there are no services of any kind at the church on that evening, and I have lived so long in the church here and done so much harm, that I am now anxious to do some good if possible. We will pay for our fuel and lights. I suppose you will have no objection to our using one of the little rooms in the basement. We could clean up the church kitchen and meet in it."

"No," said Mr. Wrong, "you can't have the church kitchen or any other part of the church in which to hold meetings on eccentric lines. I do not intend that second blessingism shall be introduced into this church or community. I am a loyal Methodist, and I intend to enforce the law. I was afraid when you went away to that camp-meeting that you would come home with a lot of nonsense in your head. Wright, you know we have always been friends, and I say to you candidly, I would not have had you to get mixed up with this holiness movement for any consideration that can be imagined. Now let me, as your best friend, advise you to drop the whole thing, and be the sober, loyal man of the church that you have always been."

With this the conversation ended, but the people

all over town were deeply interested to know what had made such a change in Wright, and as he told of the camp-meeting, and of his conversion and sanctification, many expressed a wish to attend a holiness meeting.

On the very Friday evening following the conversation between Wright and his pastor, several friends, apparently by chance, dropped in for a friendly call at Wright's house. The camp-meeting was soon under discussion, and Wright and his wife were singing some of the full salvation songs, and finding that several of their callers were in tears, they went to prayer and to their great joy had a conversion, and one sister, who had long been hungering and thirsting for righteousness, was most gloriously sanctified.

The meeting broke up with a mutual agreement that they would meet at the same place the next Friday evening for song and prayer, and so they did.

Mr. Wrong was away at the time on a visit, and before he returned the third prayer meeting had been held, and some half dozen sinners had been converted, and four or five believers had been sanctified. When Mr. Wrong got home and heard of these meetings at Mr. Wright's house, he was full of indignation. He at once wrote to Dr. Stuffy, his presiding elder, and advised him of the lawless state of things that existed in his church. "This thing must be

stopped at once," said Wrong, "or there is no telling whereunto it will grow, and I will tear this
church to its mudsills and take my chances of
rebuilding it out of sound material, rather than
have this plague of holiness sweep in among us."

Dr. Stuffy wrote the following letter to Mr. Wrong:

"*My Dear Brother Wrong:* Your letter just received.
You have my most hearty approval in your purpose
to stamp out the very beginnings of the holiness
movement in your charge.

"We now see the wisdom of our great church in
giving our pastors such absolute control over the laity.

"The law gives you authority to stop this man
from holding these meetings in his home, and you
should do it at once. I will be down next week.

"P. S.—The president of PeaRidge College, where
I have been trying to get your degree of divinity,
informs me that there are some expenses connected
with the conferring of the degree of D. D., and you
must send in fifteen dollars. He wanted twenty-five
dollars, but I beat him down to fifteen dollars. Send
the money just as soon as you can. With kindest
regards, Rev. Jalpock Stuffy, D. D."

Mr. Wrong was not exactly pleased with the
letter. He had hoped for a document that he could
lay before his disloyal members, but the post-script,
which was so arranged that it could not be detached,
made it impossible for him to show the letter.

He went at once to Wright's store and told him
that word had come from the presiding elder that

the prayer-meetings must stop. Poor Wright, although he had been a member of the church for a number of years, he had been in a situation not to know what was going on in church circles, and he was utterly unprepared for the turn things had taken. "Brother Wrong," said he, "do I understand you to say that there is a law in our church that gives you a right to forbid me holding a prayer-meeting in my own house with a few of my neighbors, and that, too, when it interferes with no service at the church?" "Yes, sir," said Wrong "there is such a law, and a most excellent law it is, and if properly enforced, it will bring peace back to our church, and run this holiness out of the country."

WRIGHT: "And you propose to enforce this law against me, and break up my little prayer-meeting."

WRONG: "I intend to have control of all services held in the bounds of my charge."

WRIGHT: "Will you come and take charge of our prayer-meeting?"

WRONG: "No, sir; the church is the place to hold meetings in, and I do not propose to scatter about."

WRIGHT: "You refused us the church, brother, even the church kitchen."

WRONG: "Well, those eccentric meetings must stop at once."

WRIGHT: "Brother Wrong, you are well aware

that during the three years you have been my pastor, I have been having card parties and dances at my house, and that I have gone regularly to all sorts of shows and worldly amusements, and yet you never gave me a word of admonition or warning, much less a threat of law; now that I have been converted, and sanctified, and my house has become a house of prayer, you threaten me with law and discipline. Now, is that becoming conduct in a man of God, a Methodist preacher?"

WRONG: "Oh, I never saw one of these holiness cranks who would not undertake to lecture his pastor. That is one trouble with them, they lose reverence for all *regularly constituted authority in the church.* I am a loyal Methodist myself, and I propose to enforce the law. What the General Conference says do, I will do."

WRIGHT: "But, Brother Wrong, you did not answer my question. Is it consistent for you to take my money, and eat my chicken, and let me dance and play cards without rebuke, when you knew I was a sinner, and now that I am converted and you refuse me the privilege of a little prayer-meeting in my church, built largely with my money, and I set up a prayer-meeting in my own home, you order me to stop it,—I simply ask you, is that *consistent?*"

WRONG: "The General Conference is the law-making body of our church, and it has spoken and I intend to obey to the letter. And all the bishops of the church will stand by me in the enforcement of the law."

WRIGHT: "I see that you do not intend to answer my question."

WRONG: "I will enforce the law."

And with this Mr. Wrong turned on his heel and left the store.

"What are you going to do, Wright?" said his partner, who had heard the conversation, as the preacher left the store.

WRIGHT: "Do! Continue my prayer-meeting, of course. I would lose my self-respect if I permitted a man to dictate to me in such matters. Let's get a Discipline and see if there is any such law."

The Discipline was secured and sure enough they found the paragraph, which reads as follows: "Any traveling or local preacher, or *layman* who shall hold public religious services within the bounds of any mission, circuit, or station, when requested by the preacher in charge not to hold such services, shall be guilty of imprudent conduct, and shall be dealt with as the law provides in such cases."

"There is where he gets me," said Wright. "My mind is made up, I will continue my prayer-meeting and take the consequences."

I will not weary the reader with details. The prayer-meetings were continued. Wright was brought to trial and expelled from the church. He appealed the case to the quarterly conference, and while he had the sympathy of every layman of that body, the law was plainly against him, and the decision of the lower court was affirmed. Wright wrote out a statement containing an account of what his life had been before attending the holiness camp-meeting, what a change had come to him, and what his life had been since. How that when his house was a place of revelry and sin, he was unmolested, but as soon as it became a house of prayer, he was driven from the church. The statement was refused space in the Southern Methodist organs. The independent papers published it, and the secular papers took it up and gave it to the world.

The damage which came to Southern Methodism, as a result of the enacting and enforcing of this law, can not be estimated.

The people of this "land of the free and home of the brave" are jealous of any sort of encroachment upon their liberties. Especially is this true of their religious liberties. They are ready to uphold and enforce all law that is in harmony with the just and equal regulation of society, but they are opposed to class legislation. They are not willing that burdens grievous to be borne shall be laid upon the shoulders of the many, that the few may go free of burdens and revel in luxury and ease.

And while the lay people of this great country recognize and reverence the high and holy office of the ministry, they are ready to resent and vigorously protest against any sort of attempt at ecclesiastical tyranny. Thinking men have seen enough of that sort of thing.

The effete nations of Europe, like barren fig trees, withering in their intellectual, commercial, and spiritual life, bear witness to the blasting influence of ecclesiastical tyranny.

This Protestant country does not propose to submit to it.

Especially is this true of the rank and file of Southern Methodism. While they recognize the necessity of law, and the crime of rebellion against all righteous authority, they do not intend to surrender their right to sing and pray with their friends about their own hearth stones, or to meet in the cool shade of the grove to worship God in the great camp-meetings as their fathers did before them.

CHAPTER XIX.

LAYMEN TO THE RESCUE.

The account of Mr. Wright's conversion and sanctification, and his cottage prayer-meeting, his trial and expulsion from the church, spread throughout the entire connection.

The very fact that Mr. Wright had been giving dances and card parties in his house, up to the time of his attending the holiness camp-meeting, and that without any sort of interference from his pastor, who seemed so eager to enforce the law; but as soon as scenes of revelry are changed for scenes of prayer and praise, he is expelled from the church, put the inconsistency of the methods of the anti-holiness faction in the church in so clear and unfavorable a light, it proved an eye-opener indeed. Men of highest position in the church, both ministers and laymen, lifted up their voices in solemn and vigorous protest against the new and odious law, which had been enforced against Mr. Wright.

A short time before the meeting of the General Conference, to which Huton was elected delegate, a convention of the laymen of Southern Methodism was called to meet in the city of Newton. The convention was largely attended from all parts of the connection. Many of the most prominent pastors of the church, who were in hearty sympathy with the purpose of the convention, but who feared some extreme step might be taken, were present to give wise counsel, and help to turn the current of things in the right direction.

Prominent laymen were present from every part of the church. By actual count it was found that more than one half of the lay representatives to the coming General Conference were in attendance.

The convention met in the City Hall, and when the first session was called to order the large building was packed to its utmost capacity with intelligent, serious people.

Dr. Searching, Presiding Elder of the Newton District, opened the exercises with prayer.

A bar was then fixed, and only persons who were Southern Methodist laymen, and who were in hearty sympathy with the purpose of the convention, as had been set forth in the circular calling it together, were asked to sit within the bar. Into this space something over three hundred laymen, representing every State and Territory within the bounds of Southern Methodism, took their seats, and Mr. Hicks, our lawyer friend, was introduced to make an address of welcome. Most of his speech was preserved, and will here be given to the reader as it fell from the lips of the speaker:

"*Brethren, Friends, and Fellow Methodists:* It becomes

my pleasant duty to welcome you to our beautiful little city of Newton. There has never met in this city, during my long residence in it, any body of men who were so heartily welcomed by all classes of people as you are.

"I can, in all truthfulness, say that the people were eager to entertain you. And, as you will see from this large attendance at this early hour of the first day, they are interested to know why you have met, and to see and hear what you do and say. We have met here in all good conscience, claiming to be as loyal Methodists as live within the wide bounds of our great church. I regret that some of our church papers have written against this convention, and used their influence to keep the people away from it. At this crisis in our history as a denomination it seems to me eminently proper that we should meet and counsel together. I do not like any sort of insinuation against the loyalty and integrity of laymen, simply because we are deeply solicitous for the welfare of our beloved Zion. Without boasting, I can truthfully say we have proven our faith by our works.

"Our money has erected our houses of worship, built our schools and colleges, supported our home and foreign missions, and outside of the support of our regular pastors we have patiently paid, through long decades of years, a heavy tax for the support of numerous bishops and an army of presiding elders, many of whom are of late showing a decided disposition to lord it over God's heritage. But we are not here to complain against the expenses of maintaining the church. its ministry, and the necessary machinery for the carrying forward of her enterprises and projects for the salvation and elevation of men.

"Without a living ministry to break to us the bread of life, our condition ·would be deplorable indeed. Empty our pulpits, and cease the blast of the gospel trumpet-call of warning and of mercy, and the wheels of progress would turn backward, floods of sin would flow in upon us, our homes would be desecrated, and our hopes blasted; the levers of industry would rust with disuse, the sails of commerce would flap idly in the winds, our civilization would disappear, and our posterity, a few generations hence, would be wearing breech-clouts, dwelling in huts, and living on roots.

"A living ministry, full of faith and the Holy Ghost, is the salt of the earth and the light of the world. We believe in a called ministry. We believe we ought to *support, reverence,* and *obey* the godly counsels and directions of those whom the Great Shepherd has made overseers of his flocks.

"We do not believe that the church can exist

without law, and we know that the spirit of defiance against law is wrong.   Anarchy is diabolical.

"Men who are not willing to submit to and sustain those just and equal laws for the righteous regulation and government of the Church of God, have no right to membership in the Church of God.   All reasonable men must recognize the absolute necessity of law and the enforcement of it, in order to the existence of any institution that exists for the protection and betterment of mankind.   While this is all true, nevertheless history reveals the fact that when the ministry of a church becomes secular, seeking degrees of distinction, and places of honor and wealth, that it at once becomes lax in doctrine and rigid in law, arrogant, and tyrannical in the enforcing of law.

"And it will be plain to all that a fallen, worldly clergy has never been diligent to enforce that discipline which suppresses sinful indulgences and rioting among the members of the church.   No, it will gladly take the filthy lucre of such profligates, and raise the cry of law and order against any zealous spirits who may dare to stand in the breach for the doctrines of the church and true holiness of life.

"The cry of *loyalty* is raised to disguise the spirit of persecution, while the righteous have been led to the stake, and scaffold, and the sinful have gone unwhipped of justice. Barabbas has been released, and Christ has been led away to be crucified.

"With the cry of loyalty on their lips, and the spirit of demons in their breasts, a fallen and depraved clergy have sent to martyrs' graves hundreds of thousands of the truest servants and saints of God who ever walked the paths of human life.

"These historic facts admonish us to take timely alarm when we hear well-fed and big-salaried ecclesiastics, who have no reputation for piety, raise the cry of *loyalty.*

"Loyalty to what? Loyalty to God and His eternal truths? Loyalty to original Methodism, with its separation from the world, Bible doctrines and Pentecostal baptisms? Loyalty to solemn vows to go on to perfection, and to groan after it? or loyalty to the dictates of un-Methodistic men in *doctrine* and in *life*, who have worked themselves into place and power in the Methodist Church, and propose to ignore *doctrine* and enforce *law*, until the original Methodism which blessed the multitudes of our race has been swept from the earth? (Loud applause.)

"Sad and strange as it may seem, it is nevertheless true, that in the ministry of our church there is a large class of men, elegantly arrayed in broadcloth, decorated in silk hats, stationed in city churches, drawing large salaries, and feasting sumpt-

uously every day, their names lengthened with a
couple of D's unworthily bestowed, who have joined
themselves together by a sort of common consent to
either drive the Wesleyan doctrine of sanctification
from the church, or else drive from the church those
who believe and teach it to the multitudes, who are
ever ready to congregate themselves to hear these
grand old truths proclaimed. With these facts looking us full in the face, it occurs to me that the times
are fully ripe for a convention of Methodist laymen.
(Applause.)

"Are we ready to sit quietly and see the foundations torn from under us? (Cries of "No" all over
the hall.) What do these gentlemen, who would
teach our children to ridicule Wesley and the doc
trines he preached with such signal power and bless
ing, propose to offer us for the glorious Bible truths
they propose to take from us? One of them informs
us that we are sanctified before we are converted;
another one avers that we are sanctified when we
are converted; another says that we are sanctified
at the resurrection, and still another declares that
sanctification simply means chastity, that all chaste
people are sanctified. Such jargon would have been
unworthy Balaam's *Ass*, when he opened his mouth
and rebuked the madness of the prophet. (Laughter.)
It will be noticed also that these opposers of Bible
and Methodist doctrine can no more agree with

each other than they can agree with the fathers and founders of Methodism. Whatever else this convention of laymen may do, or fail to do, it is to be hoped that the church at large will be thoroughly aroused to the fact that these 'Loyalty' howlers and holiness camp-meeting opposers are not the true shepherds of the Methodist flock. They do not increase the flock; *no one is converted under their ministry.*

"They do not lead the flock into green pastures; *no one is perfected in love under their teachings.*

"They only take the fleece, and turn the flock out, and turn with them a hungry pack of ravening wolves of *new theories* of sanctification. (Applause.)

"Suppose we give up the doctrines contained in our standards, Discipline, and Hymn-book, which one of these new theories are we to adopt? Would it not be well for these men who propose to discard Wesley to formulate something tangible among themselves to offer us in the stead of what we have, before they turn us out of the church? (Applause.)

"My brethren, pardon me for having kept you so long. I congratulate you that you have taken this good work in hand; having put your hands to the plow, do not look back, and let me exhort you with all the earnestness of my soul, whatever may come in the stormy times just ahead of us, do not cease your fight for the right, 'and don't give up the ship.'" (Volleys of "Amens" made the hall ring and tremble.)

When Mr. Hicks sat down men hurried from every part of the hall to shake his hand and thank him for his speech.

I will not weary the reader with the details of this convention. It was in session five days. The program was as follows: Prayer and testimony meeting from eight to nine; convention work from nine to twelve; preaching at half-past two; committee meetings from four to six; address, or sermon every evening.

The following addresses were prepared by committees appointed for the purpose, and ordered printed, one hundred thousand of each, to be spread broadcast over the land: An address to the bishops, one to presiding elders and pastors, and one to local preachers and laymen. We have neither time nor space to copy these addresses.

They were all short and to the point. The fact that a crisis had come in the history of the church was made plain. Bishops were urged to use their influence to lift up a high spiritual standard, and to curb the impetuous spirit of persecution on the part of the Zinzindorfian element in the church.

Presiding elders were assured that there was no spirit of rebellion on the part of the laity, at the same time no sort of a spirit of tyranny could or would be tolerated, and the office of presiding elder could only remain in the church so long as the incumbents of said office were men of *piety*, and intelligence, such as would commend them as leaders of the people, sent of God, full of faith and the Holy Ghost.

Pastors were assured of the hearty sympathy and support of the people, and urged to inculcate the old Bible truths preached by the founders of the church, and to purge the church of worldliness.

Local preachers and laymen were exhorted, while they should guard religious liberty as one of the most sacred gems of freedom, they should be careful to avoid any sort of reckless disregard of legitimate law; to remain true and steadfast to God and their church, to claim every *right*, and to discharge every *duty* in reverence, love, and fear. Faithful warning was given against all ungodly strife, or come-outism, and the old Methodist books were heartily recommended to the people for thoughtful reading.

The convention closed just before the meeting of the General Conference. The spirit of love and peace, at the same time of most dauntless courage, pervaded the entire session.

The Zinzindorfian element that has swept into Southern Methodism, and has gone forward with such reckless disregard of doctrine or law, in trampling out the old and saving truths of original Methodism, awoke to the fact that at last the true sons of Wesley were fully aroused, and stood in solid and unwavering ranks for the coming conflict.

It appeared to them at last that the work of tearing away the foundations of Methodism would prove a more difficult task than they had suspected, and not a few of them were eager to know what stand the bishops would take under the new aspect of affairs, that they might arrange accordingly.

CHAPTER XX.

THE GENERAL CONFERENCE.

Never in the history of Methodism had a General Conference assembled in which there was centered so much interest. The anti-Wesleyan element in the conference was strong, and past successes in fighting the holiness movement had made them bold and aggressive.

First, their fight had been made against local preachers and camp-meetings. All thoughtful men knew that their real war was against the doctrine and experience of entire sanctification.

To have made an open fight against that doctrine would have been a hazardous enterprise. Many true patriots do not know how much they love their flag, until it is fired on by an enemy. Then all their country love flames up in their breasts, and they are ready to do and die.

So it is with Methodists. They are a liberal people. They will work with you in union meetings, baptize you as you choose, commune with all who permit them, but make an open attack upon one of the cardinal doctrines of Methodism, and they are ready to meet you, Bible in hand. Had the anti-holiness people in the Methodist Church made an open attack upon the doctrine of entire sanctifica-tion in Annual and General conferences, thousands of Methodists would have rallied to the defense, and the enemy would have gone down before overwhelming numbers who would have stood firmly for the original doctrines of the church. But the enemy has always fought from cover.

When they raised the cry of "new heresy," they soon found out their mistake, changed their tactics, admitted that sanctification was a doctrine of the church, "but these evangelists are a disturbing element." Then the war was extended to all local preachers, and then it took in active laymen.

Then the batteries of the opposition were leveled against the holiness camp-meetings. No tent revival escaped them. Even a group of people assembled in a cottage at night to read, and pray, and testify to the baptism of the Holy Ghost could not escape these men who had set themselves to hunt down and drive from the church the Methodist doctrine of full salvation.

Meantime there had been much manipulation in the making of appointments in Annual conferences, and the holiness revival was struck a blow at every possible opportunity.

At this General Conference the Zinzindorfian wing in the Methodist camp had massed its forces, to strike a more direct blow at pastors and laymen who were in any way in sympathy with the holiness movement. And while they were fully aware of the convention having met in Newton, and that from it there had gone out an influence which had a tendency to arouse the church to the defense of the old Wesleyan doctrine, at the same time, full of arrogance, always a characteristic of men engaged in religious persecution, they had come to look with such contempt on the people whom they denominated "second blessingists," that they, now that they were together, gave the convention but little thought.

The reader is not concerned to know much of the routine work of the conference, and we will not detain him, but hasten to that part of the work done by the body in which we are all especially interested.

It was the purpose of the opposition to put into the Discipline a paragraph that would forbid laymen attending the holiness camp-meetings, or taking any part in them, that would also shut out of our pulpits all holiness evangelists, and that would greatly hinder pastors in sympathy with the holiness movement in the work of promoting revivals.

It was the purpose of the *true Methodist* element of the body to call the attention of the conference from the enacting of *law* to the protecting of *doctrine*. Many speeches had been made by the opposition before Huton could get the floor. All sorts of false charges had been brought against the holiness people, laying at their door all the blame for the strife and confusion in the church, on the subject of doctrine, and urging the necessity of a law that would "suppress the revival in the church, or drive it out of the church," as one of the champions expressed it. As usual, *law, law,* was the cry of the enemies of the holiness revival.

Finally Huton got the recognition of the chairman, and the vast audience, who had learned who he was, and something of his history, in perfect silence, riveted its eyes upon him.

I wish I could give Huton's speech in full, but limited space forbids. His first sentence was:

"*Mr. Chairman,* It seems to me, sir. that we are in imminent danger of having too much *law,* and too little *gospel.*" He continued: "For some years past there has been a strong tendency in our church to magnify *law,* and minify *doctrine.*

"In this matter we have doubtless fallen into a grave and dangerous error. When we surrender the great doctrines that brought us into existence as a church, and endued us with power from on high for service, I care not what our laws are, our ship will run upon the rocks of unbelief, and be beaten to pieces by the breakers of worldliness. Already there are vast thousands of our people who do not know what to believe, and floods of worldliness are pouring in upon us from every quarter. It seems to me that if, as a church, we are sound in doctrine, and holy in life, it will be very easy to enact simple and just laws for our government. It is not hard to govern a family where all the children love the parents supremely, and love each other unselfishly.

"Let Methodist people be taught the doctrine and led into the experience of perfect love, and we shall not need much law, and what we do need will be enacted and enforced, not by a faction with a concealed end in view, but by the common, mutual, and peaceful consent of the entire Methodist family.

"I believe there is a majority on this conference floor who believe the time has come when it is not more *machinery* we need, but more *power* to run the machinery we have.

"This country is not suffering for more *ecclesiasticism*, it is more *evangelism* we need. (Applause.)

"Our people, and I well know whereof I speak, are crying out, not for new laws, enacted in a partisan spirit, that one element in the church may oppress and dictate to another, no, sir; it is the old Methodist doctrine of full salvation from sin that our people are clamoring for.

"Between the old doctrines that our founders and fathers preached, and the new laws that an anti-Wesleyan element in this body have made, and would make, there is all the difference that there is between *bread* and *stone*. (Loud applause.)

"The people are asking for *bread*, will you give them a *stone?* (Applause.)

"The charge has been made on this floor that the

strife which exists in our church to-day is all because of that element of people in the church known as the holiness people. I deny the charge *in toto.*

"The holiness people believe in, and are true to those doctrines of the church which differentiate us from other bodies of Christians, and in spite of the Zinzindorfianism and worldliness that has come into our church, they have tried hard to keep the original fire, which came from heaven in the days of the immortal Wesley, burning on Methodist altars. (Applause.)

"I grant you that they have contended earnestly for the faith once delivered to the Methodists, but the disturbance and strife has come from the other side in this struggle to maintain Methodist teachings in Methodist pulpits.

"Permit me, with all due respect for our chief pastors, to say that the fountain out of which the stream of strife has flown through all the church, was an unfortunate paragraph in the Bishop's address delivered to this body in the year 1894. In that address our chief pastors highly commend the doctrine of entire sanctification. They say let 'the doctrine be *preached* and the experience be *testified.*'

"But they also make a most unwarranted attack upon the holiness people, the only people on the earth who are preaching and testifying the doctrine, bringing accusations against them, which can not possibly be sustained, and suggesting a method of procedure that, if carried out, is bound to precipitate the whole church into a state of turmoil and strife. Strange to say, notwithstanding the fact that the General Conference refused to make such a law as the bishops suggested, the anti-holiness element in the church proceeded as if the law had been enacted, and when remonstrated with by their persecuted brethren, they referred them to the Bishops' Address, as if it were the law of the church.

"The result has been sad indeed. The very men who have raised the cry of 'loyalty' walked rough shod over law, and have turned and driven out from the church many of our best and truest people.

"But the most alarming feature of the situation is the fact that all of this lawlessness on the part of those who would make us believe that they are the 'truly loyal,' has met with no rebuke or censure from those who are high in authority in the church, but, on the other hand, has met with sympathy and assistance. ("True!" "true!" came from every part of the audience.)

"Now, my brethren, hear me. I do not speak unadvisedly, or under excitement. I have made it my business to study the situation carefully. I have traveled extensively throughout the length and breadth of our wide connection. I know the feeling of the great masses of the people. I have talked and prayed over these matters with the most intellectual men in our church, and I stand in my place to-day to say to you that we have reached a crisis in the history of Southern Methodism.

"We, who believe in and teach the original doctrines of the Wesleys, do not intend to leave the church, we do not intend to be driven out of it.

"*Mark my words well.* We do not intend to be further harassed by unjust enactments, to hinder and embarass us in the greatest work in the world. the securing of the conversion of sinners and the sanctification of believers. We have rights. we have suffered them to be encroached upon until patience has ceased to be a virtue; they shall be trampled under foot no longer, and here and now we demand that all aggressive movement against the doctrine of entire sanctification shall cease, or we will ask for a division of the church." (Loud applause and great excitement followed.)

When quiet was restored, Huton continued: "We do not make these statements without first having made sure of the ground beneath our feet. We have been in counsel with the best legal minds in this nation, and we are ready, after years of patient suffering, waiting, and praying, to make the issue. (Applause.) I am personally acquainted with more than half of the members of this body, and I do not hesitate to say our minds are made up. The motion that has been offered here, which, if it become a law, would infringe upon the rights of our people, both clerical and lay, and is intended to interfere with and hinder the progress of the holiness revival, must be withdrawn, or there will be offered a resolution on this floor, in less than twenty-four hours, looking to the division of the church." (Amen, Amen, Amen, rang out from all over the building.)

The hour of adjournment had come. The gavel fell upon the table with Huton's last sentence. As the people poured like a great stream out of the large building where the conference was being held, excitement was suppressed, the true sons of Wesley were radiant with joy, but the Zinzindorfians were white with disappointment and rage. They knew that their cause had gone down in disaster.

I must not detain the reader with detail. The objectional m o t i o n was withdrawn. *Methodism* reigned supreme throughout the remainder of the session, the revival spirit was on the people, powerful sermons on full salvation were preached in many pulpits, and "The old time religion is good enough for me," was sung with an unusual spirit and unction.

The conference wisely concluded that they needed no new bishops, but took pains to see to it that all the connectional officers were of the true Wesleyan Methodist type. It was the dawn of a new and glorious era in the history of Southern Methodism.

CHAPTER XXI.

THE CLOSING CHAPTER.

As the news of the victory won for truth and righteousness at the General Conference spread throughout the church, there was great joy among the people. For twenty years the enemy had been in the saddle. Sound doctrine had been sadly discounted, and the principal aim of those in power had been to think out, enact, and enforce law that would enable them to suppress the revival of the doctrine and experience of entire sanctification. Under this regime of conflicting theories, neglect of and opposition to Methodist doctrines, the church had been flooded with worldliness and un-Methodistic teachings. In many of our pulpits there were men of shallow learning, and æsthetical tastes, with long and high-sounding titles, who knew and cared almost nothing of Methodism in its original purity and power. Under their rosewater essays there was not, could not be conviction for sin, much less the manifestation of the Spirit's power in regeneration and sanctification.

It almost makes one weep when he thinks how these ecclesiastical fops had been petted by those in authority, and transferred from one good paying station to another, to shear the sheep and turn them over to the wolves of unsound doctrine and worldliness. When the turn in the tide of affairs came, and under the new administration the spiritual life of the church began to deepen and quicken, these gentlemen awoke to the fact that their culture and tastes better fitted them for the pulpits of the Episcopal church, and quite a procession of shining plug hats and long-tailed cloth coats, curving gracefully in the evening breezes, marched over to the Episcopalians. It was a good ridance.

Not a few dancing, card-playing members of our church, who had well nigh exhausted all of their physical strength running first to this ball, then to that show, or card party, and then to the church festival, thought it would be so nice to have *forty days of lent each year in which one could rest one's self from the merry whirls of the exhaustive enjoyments of society.* Besides ingenious minds had sought out a number of little, innocent parlor games with which to amuse the dear people during the humiliations and devotions of the lenten season. Then they could not afford to be worried about the sinfulness of sin, and the importance of a pure heart, and so over they went to the Episcopalians. The reader will be interested to know that Sister Dishrattier was one of this number. She bought herself a very high bonnet, and a very large prayer-book, a large supply of face powder, and a pug dog, and took her proper place in society.　The stiffness with which she would strut past Central Church on Sabbath mornings made the sexton stare after her in wonder.

There had accumulated in the conference quite a number of preachers who ranked about third class. They had done little for years, except chew and smoke tobacco, eat chickens, and fight holiness. Now it was manifest to all that these brethren were without a job.　The Episcopalians would not have them, the Reformers did not want them, and so they came down out of Methodist pulpits, where they had never had a right to be, and went their way, one to his field, and another to his merchandise.

Dr. Gall had for some years been hanging on to the conference, waiting for the maturity of a " twenty year plan " life insurance policy.　It came at an opportune moment for him, for the church had fully determined that he and his large class should no longer fill the presiding eldership.　Dr. Gall was superannuated, and went on to a little farm near Newton, where he spent some years very comfortably. Some friend sent him the PENTECOSTAL HERALD. and, strange to say, the old doctor's prejudices subsided, he became interested in the biographies of the old Methodists, and finally became a regular camper at the Huton Holiness Camp-meetings, and was greatly blessed and much loved by the holiness people.

Dr. Poolkins was not a success as a lecturer.　He

was made president of a little college, located somewhere in the backwoods, and took charge of the
institution with the usual flourish of trumpets, held
the position for a few years, but saw it was going to
die on his hands, and resigned. He was then agent
for a patent wire fence of some kind for a while, but
when the General Conference met, of which we have
written, he was on a small district, where he had been
placed in order that he might harrass the holiness
people, and if possible kill a couple of holiness camp-
meetings which sprung up within its bounds. The
doctor made poor headway. The next fall, while at
the Annual Conference, he received a telegram calling him to the deathbed of his wife's father.

On finding that the old gentleman had left Mrs.
Poolkins a snug little farm, some Jersey cows, and a
few thousand dollars in cash, the doctor telegraphed
at once to the bishop who was holding the con-
ence that his *throat was so sore* he feared to take
work and asked to be located. His request was
granted, without a dissenting vote. It was soon
quite manifest that many men who had had much
to say about "*loyalty*" were Methodist only in name,
and one way and another they soon disappeared
from the ranks of our ministry.

Mr. Hicks continued the practice of law, spending
much of the winter season in missionary work among
the neglected people of the city, and during the

summer months rendering valuable assistance in establishing and conducting camp-meetings.

There were constant calls for Huton to assist in revival meetings in all parts of the church, and after carefully weighing the matter he located, that he might devote his entire time to evangelistic work.

There was a most remarkable change in the yearly sessions of the annual conferences. They became seasons of genuine revival. The bishops urged the people to "go on to perfection." Frequently revivals would break out in annual conferences and spread throughout the churches embraced within the conference limits.

And it came to pass that you could attend an annual conference and not see a preacher smoking or chewing tobacco, or hear one word uttered against the doctrine or experience of entire sanctification.

[THE END.]